ECONOMIC LIFE IN THE REAL WORLD

Economic Life in the Real World

Logic, Emotion and Ethics

CHARLES STAFFORD

London School of Economics and Political Science

CAMBRIDGE
UNIVERSITY PRESS

University Printing House, Cambridge CB2 8BS, United Kingdom

One Liberty Plaza, 20th Floor, New York, NY 10006, USA

477 Williamstown Road, Port Melbourne, VIC 3207, Australia

314–321, 3rd Floor, Plot 3, Splendor Forum, Jasola District Centre,
New Delhi – 110025, India

79 Anson Road, #06-04/06, Singapore 079906

Cambridge University Press is part of the University of Cambridge.

It furthers the University's mission by disseminating knowledge in the pursuit of
education, learning, and research at the highest international levels of excellence.

www.cambridge.org
Information on this title: www.cambridge.org/9781108483216
DOI: 10.1017/9781108673426

First published 2020

A catalogue record for this publication is available from the British Library.

Library of Congress Cataloging-in-Publication Data
Names: Stafford, Charles, author.
Title: Economic life in the real world : logic, emotion and ethics /
Charles Stafford, London School of Economics.
Description: New York : Cambridge University Press, 2020. | Series: New
departures in anthropology | Includes bibliographical references and
index.
Identifiers: LCCN 2019032205 | ISBN 9781108483216 (hardback) | ISBN
9781108716550 (paperback) | ISBN 9781108483216 (ebook)
Subjects: LCSH: Economics--Psychological aspects. | Human behavior.
Classification: LCC HB74.P8 S73 2020 | DDC 330.01/9--dc23
LC record available at https://lccn.loc.gov/2019032205

ISBN 978-1-108-48321-6 Hardback
ISBN 978-1-108-71655-0 Paperback

Dedicated to E. W. F. Linfoot

Contents

Preface

This book is an exploration of the psychology of everyday economic life, written by an anthropologist who has carried out long-term fieldwork in rural China and Taiwan. It is also an attempt – not the first one, of course – to bring anthropology, psychology and economics into some kind of conversation. On the surface, this shouldn't be too huge a task. Anthropology, psychology and economics are three human science disciplines. They share a good deal in terms of their intellectual origins and their contemporary subject matter. Of particular relevance to this book is their shared interest in moral aspects of economic agency, including the question of whether ours is a fundamentally cooperative or fundamentally selfish species. Much of the time, however, scholars in these academic fields live on very different planets. In fact, anthropologists could be said to pay quite a lot of attention to economists, but this attention manifests itself in an odd way. The former are sharply critical of the latter, while having little understanding of what they actually do in their work and of the Utilitarian tradition that helped inspire this. Meanwhile, it sometimes feels as if half the economists in the world would like to turn themselves into psychologists – albeit not in a way that every psychologist would credit – while the other half are running in the opposite direction.

This complex state of affairs is not going to be resolved by one book, not least because there are political undercurrents to it. For a number of reasons, including its historical links to colonialism, anthropology has become an intrinsically radical discipline. So far as most of today's anthropologists are concerned, to take economics seriously is tantamount to endorsing global capitalism. (I presume that Marx, a keen student of economics, would have found this a baffling inference.) To take psychology seriously also has political implications for anthropologists, although the discussion of this is usually more muted.

Speaking personally, I was attracted to anthropology because of its intrinsic radicalism. In this respect, I have not changed. But I differ from most of my colleagues in believing that we have much to learn from economists and, especially, from psychologists. This is, in part, because I am a universalist of a kind. As this book illustrates, I have spent my career studying cultural-historical particulars by means of participant observation fieldwork. At one point, for instance, I became intrigued by popular Chinese practices related to number – some of which, such as seeking lottery numbers from the gods, really captured my attention as an outsider. And yet I now believe that variation *within* societies, e.g. between people of different social 'kinds', is in some respects more interesting – and may ultimately be more important – than variation *between* societies. As a corollary of this, I am more open than most anthropologists to universalist accounts of human nature. In short, I do agree that there might be such a thing. This is a big confession for an anthropologist, and it gives me something in common with at least some economists and some psychologists.

As anthropologists see things, universalist accounts of human nature – not least the recent attempts by cognitive and evolutionary psychologists to explain 'how humans think' – make a grave error in downplaying history and culture, the two distinctive features of actual human experience in the world. As an extension of this, they hold that such accounts are not nearly political enough or even that they can be politically dangerous, i.e. when they slip towards crude biological determinism, and even racism. When it comes to their own work, anthropologists prefer to keep the focus firmly on questions of culture and history and politics, carefully avoiding any questions of evolved psychology. As a consequence, however, we are left in a curious position. For there is surely nothing more politically significant, in the end, than the relationship between human psychology and human history. Indeed, it is *only* by virtue of our psychology – that is, by virtue of 'how humans think' – that we can become the kind of historical agents we are: the kind entangled in sociality and shared intentions from start to finish. Anthropological attacks on psychologism are thus misguided, as I see it. In fact, anthropology is well placed to make a major contribution to psychology, precisely by making it much more anthropological. In order for this to happen, however, a number of entrenched scholarly biases on all sides would have to be overcome.

* * *

At the time of my first fieldwork in rural Taiwan in the mid-1980s, it was still just about possible to take China and Taiwan as exemplars of 'communism' and 'capitalism', respectively. Even back then, however, doing this was far from straightforward. China was embracing market principles and rapidly moving away from collectivism proper. This took place under very particular circumstances, of course, and Mao's legacies could still be seen everywhere one looked, even long after Deng Xiaoping's famous southern tour in 1992 (indeed, even now). And yet, to state the obvious, today's global capitalism would look radically different were China to be suddenly taken out of the equation. Meanwhile, Taiwan's own experience of rapid economic development – its post-war 'miracle', which came much sooner than the Chinese one – also took place under very particular circumstances. This was capitalism, to be sure. And yet the Kuomintang (KMT) government played a major role in Taiwan's economy for years (they actually owned a high proportion of commercial enterprises), and there was substantial backing from the United States as part of a broader Cold War strategy for containing communism. This wasn't just a story of free markets.

In any case, neither the people I met in rural Taiwan nor those I subsequently met in rural China, when I started doing fieldwork there a few years later, have been the main beneficiaries of the economic transformations taking place around them. They were (and mostly still are) at the margins and sometimes openly exploited. And yet quite a few of them have been excited about, indeed have felt liberated by, small-scale entrepreneurial activities of various kinds and the making of money. Moreover, most rural people that I have met – in both places – think of economic success as an *ethical* imperative: something to be pursued for family and communal purposes rather than selfish ones. Just for this reason, when it comes to strategising about economic life, the stakes for them are high and the emotions engaged. In short, they experience the economy not only as a domain of logical deliberation but also as one of emotions – and certainly as one of ethics.

Against this background, I have sometimes felt that life under the radically different, if now converging, political economies of China and Taiwan is surprisingly similar for the people I have come to know in both places, even though it is easy to list ways in which it is not. Their shared 'Chineseness', however contentious, plays a part in this, as does their shared distance from the world of urban elites. But so too, I want to suggest, does the fact that they share a *species essence*, to use the old Marxist formulation. As humans, we have no choice but to cooperate with others – kin and non-kin – because we are an essentially social species. This sets the conditions for exploitation and generates a lot of unhappiness everywhere, so far as I know. It certainly does in rural China and Taiwan. It also sets the conditions for learning and more specifically for human self-education, as I will discuss in this book. This can be liberating. For better or worse, however, the one thing we really cannot liberate ourselves from is our species essence.

* * *

In spite of significant overlap in their subject matter, the disciplines of anthropology, psychology and economics have radically different ways of approaching lived reality. Model-building economists have been accused, in recent years, of having lost touch with it altogether – a charge they find intensely frustrating, for reasons I will explain. Psychologists, as they go about doing their experiments and surveys, worry that even relatively minor biases in their sampling of reality might distort the results they end up with, leading them to draw exactly the wrong conclusions. Compared to model-building economists – who are allowed to play with any assumption they like – psychologists seem obsessed with getting reality right. By contrast, no ethnographic sample of reality can ever be said to be biased per se, so far as most anthropologists are concerned. The question is what conclusions we draw, and what interpretations we make, based on the sample we happen to end up with. And yet a colleague once told me, in semi-jest, that she always felt a bit anxious on the rare occasions during fieldwork when she walked over to the next village. Might the people there contradict everything she believed to be true about the society she was studying?

My own research in China and Taiwan has involved a good deal of moving around. Since the mid-1980s, I have done fieldwork in five different places: two rural communities in Taiwan (Angang on the eastern side and South Bridge on the western side), two rural communities in China (Dragon Head in the north-east and Protected Mountain in the south-west) and one small Chinese town/city (Western Cliff, in the north-east). The people I have met in these places – and in nearby towns and cities – are a varied group: fishermen and farmers, teachers and students, government employees and entrepreneurs. Actually, I have also met accountants, postmen, full-time grandparents, calligraphers (and artists of other kinds), hairdressers, funeral troupe performers, betel nut sellers ... the list goes on. It's a fascinating sample, in fact – or at least I've personally been fascinated by the stories these people have been so generous in sharing. Indeed, one thing I learned from doing fieldwork is that rural life is a good deal more diverse and complicated and interesting than many urban people tend to assume, one feature of this being that much of the Chinese and Taiwanese countryside has now been semi-urbanised, with all that this implies. Be that as it may, the people I've met *do* primarily come from rural backgrounds and they also come from what their compatriots would think of as relatively traditional backgrounds. It is not that they live in ahistorical bubbles, far from it. Still, they are from villages and towns where kinship connections remain a major fact of life, for most people, and where activities such as gift exchange and religious rituals help bind individuals into enduring social units.

Readers familiar with modern China and Taiwan may thus wonder how representative the observations in this book can be, based as they are on research among a handful of people in the countryside, most of whom appear to be tradition-oriented in one sense or another. After all, isn't *change* the thing that drives so many of us to want to study East Asia today? I have two reactions to this. First, I would want to assert – based on my wider experience of life in China and Taiwan – that what I have learned in the countryside remains deeply relevant across the board in these two societies. Indeed, far from being irrelevant to how most people there live now, I would argue that rural ethnography gives us a great opportunity to study – on a manageable scale, and thus holistically – the core issues, such as planning for the future and grappling with human cooperation, that continue to absorb Chinese and Taiwanese people wherever they may live. My second reaction is that my goal as an anthropologist, in any case, has *never* been to study a particular culture or society. I have never really thought of myself as a China or Taiwan expert. What interests me is how the anthropological study of a group of people, living anywhere, can illuminate broad questions about the nature of human experience. I am confident that the people I have lived alongside during fieldwork in the countryside are perfectly good representatives of humanity as a whole, and that is the spirit in which this book has been written.

Acknowledgements

I am deeply grateful to the people of Angang, Dragon Head, South Bridge, Protected Mountain and Western Cliff for the incredible kindness they have shown me during my stays in their communities. I am also grateful to the many colleagues and students in the United Kingdom, Taiwan, China and elsewhere who have helped me as I tried to improve my ideas and my understandings. In particular, I would like to thank colleagues and research students in the Department of Social Anthropology at Cambridge University, including James Laidlaw in particular. A couple of years ago, I gave a version of Chapter 5 (the self-education chapter) at their Senior Seminar, and their thoughtful and helpful reaction to it gave me the confidence I needed to finish writing this long-overdue book. I should note that Chapter 4 (the one that compares Robert Lucas's account of learning and economic growth to some fieldwork data from Taiwan) is a heavily revised version of a Chinese-language article entitled 'Scales of Economy: Some Lessons from a Case-Study in Taiwan'. This was published in *China Studies* by Nanjing University in 2006. Many thanks to my wonderful NJU colleague, Professor Yang Der-ruey, for permission to publish it here, as well as for his friendship and help over the years. Finally, much love to A, to B, and especially to E – to whom the book is dedicated.

ONE

Introduction

During the fall and winter of 2000 to 2001, I lived for several months in a rural township in far south-western China. I soon learned that this rather beautiful place, which I call Protected Mountain, had an interesting economic history.[1] In the late Qing and early Republican eras, a number of people from that area moved across the nearby border to Burma (Myanmar), where some of them became successful traders. At the time, this was explicitly seen a *moral* achievement – a way of bringing glory to the ancestors – and the typical pattern was that 'Chinese sojourners' (*huaqiao*) of this kind would eventually return, at least in death, to Protected Mountain, where they and their families had built the large courtyard houses and ancestral temples that dot the landscape to the present day.

Life since then has not always been good, however. Mao's revolution upended China's social and moral certainties. It was notably hard on businesspeople, on families with international connections and on those who revered Confucian ideals – all three being common in the particular case of Protected Mountain. Fortunes were lost, and during the years of high Maoism most tokens of wealth and culture, including

---

[1] In order to protect the privacy of the people I have met during fieldwork, all place and personal names in this book have been changed. I have also sometimes changed identifying personal details (such as family size or occupation), but only where the details do not matter in a substantive way for the particular points I am making.

decorative flourishes on homes and temples, were either destroyed or hidden away (sometimes literally covered up with mud). Later on, once the post-Mao era of socioeconomic reforms had taken hold, attempts were made to revive the local economy, in part on the back of dormant cultural practices. Houses and temples were rebuilt, and, as elsewhere in China, the standard of living gradually improved. And yet when I stayed there, the township primarily evoked, at least for me, a kind of faded grandeur: a sense that *very* good economic news was mostly a thing of the past.

Rather than focus on this long narrative of economic rise and fall, however, I want to draw your attention to a quickly passing moment, a single economic transaction. This took place in front of Protected Mountain's most visible public temple, the Temple of Learning (*wenmiao*), which is approached by a stone walkway rising out of the surrounding fields. At the bottom of this, in the mornings and afternoons, it is common to find at least one person trying to sell something.

One weekday, a Chinese friend and I came upon a young girl and boy, about eight and ten years old respectively, standing there selling bunches of small, green bananas from a trolley. The price, they said, was 7 mao per jin. In truth, we were more concerned with the large size of the bunches than with the negligible price (roughly 20 US cents per kilogram at the time). We wanted a few bananas. Couldn't they cut a bunch in half for us? No, the boy replied, claiming not to have a knife. Unimpressed by this level of customer service, my friend made a mildly sarcastic remark, and we left.

Later, however – having walked past someone selling bananas for twice as much – we did go back and buy some from the children. These were weighed on a scale and came to a little more than 3 jin. Now was the moment for the boy, who seemed to be in charge, to tell us the price, presumably reckoned at 3-and-a-bit jin times 7 mao. But he went blank and turned to the younger girl beside him to anxiously whisper, *duoshou?* – 'How much?' The girl stared at the ground.

At this point, my friend's attitude changed. He became noticeably warmer towards the children, told them what to charge us and even gave them a suggestion or two about dealing with customers. Then we left with our bananas and walked up the steep path towards the Temple of Learning.

* * *

What can this story, this anecdote, tell us? If nothing else, it reminds us that economic life is *psychological*. In buying and selling things, we rely on cognitive skills. Sellers of bananas ought to know a little bit about calculation (even if they sometimes do not). We also rely on the possession of information of various kinds. It helps to know, for instance, that one vendor is selling something we want for half the price of another (although, of course, this is exactly the kind of thing we often do not know). Putting our (imperfect) knowledge and skills together, we should be in a position to at least *try* to act logically[2] in the pursuit of our interests.

As the story also reminds us, however, economic life is emotional. We may buy something because we end up feeling sorry for the children who are selling it. (In the incident just described, the fact that they were not in school on a weekday indicates that they were almost certainly from a poor background.) Or we may refuse to buy from them, even to our own detriment, if they manage to offend us, however slightly, in the course of a transaction – e.g. by not cutting a bunch of bananas in half. Nor is it always easy to distinguish the logical and the emotional dimensions of economic life, much of which takes place, after all, in the company of people we *care* about in some way – e.g. our parents, siblings or friends. Indeed, total strangers in a marketplace may cause us to blush with anger, embarrassment or confusion. We care about them too,

---

[2] As will be explained in Chapter 2, I use the word 'logical' (and variations on it) in this book in preference to the word 'rational' (and variations on it) when referring to the everyday economic activity of my research interlocutors.

it seems, and are quick to pass (moral and ethical) judgement if we feel their behaviour is out of line.

But if economic life is 'psychological' in these different senses – that is, because it entails such things as knowing, feeling, calculating and judging – a crucial point follows on from this. In order for us to *have* psychological attributes, dispositions and skills of the kinds we deploy in the flow of economic life, we must have *acquired* them in some way. Of course, they might at least in part be evolutionary gifts: things that we naturally possess. This has been suggested, for example, of the basic cognitive skills that underpin human numeracy (and thus our ability to reckon prices during sales transactions) and of the basic moral dispositions that we bring to exchange (e.g. an evolved preference for 'fairness').[3] But perhaps a more intuitive answer, for most of us, is that these things come to us from experience. We gain the skills we need for the jobs we happen to be doing. We learn what counts as a 'fair trade' in the places where we happen to live. We figure out how much we personally value certain objects and experiences in the world around us. Then again, exactly how *do* we become skilled? What *is* it that makes us care about fairness? Why *do* we end up valuing some objects and experiences more than others? The developmental processes that, over time, produce these real-world outcomes are surely incredibly complicated – not only psychologically but also socially and culturally.

One complication, and the starting point for this book, is that the cognitive environments in which we as humans live are always historical – without exception. A girl in Protected Mountain may be good at calculation, and thus at reckoning prices, because her parents (so it happened) could afford to send her to school, and moreover at an historical moment when the basic level of schooling provision was adequate. (During the Cultural Revolution, schooling of any kind

---

[3] For an evolutionary account of human numeracy, see Dehaene (1997). For an evolutionary account of human morality, with a particular focus on 'fairness morality', see Baumard et al. (2013).

might not have been available to her.) If they could *not* afford to do this, however, she might instead learn 'street maths' while selling things on weekdays. In either case, as part of growing up she will encounter many specifically *Chinese* ideas, values and practices related to economic life – e.g. the idea that an agreed price, in addition to being agreeable, ought to 'sound good' (*haoting*, roughly meaning that it should be auspicious). And then all of the factors that have impinged, in some way, on her development as an economic agent – including her family's socioeconomic standing; the way maths is taught in Chinese schools (or on the streets); and the culturally specific ideas, values and practices to be found in her cognitive environment – are bound to change, some of them radically, over time.

It is certainly true, in the case of Protected Mountain, that both 'learning' and 'economy' – as well as the many connections between them – have to be understood as *historical* phenomena: saturated with meanings from a long trajectory of effort, conflict and change. Thus it is that my story about a passing sales transaction involving two children in front of the Temple of Learning is directly linked to the much longer story with which I began: the one about the rise and fall of families and communities along the Burma frontier.

* * *

As my willingness to dwell on such stories suggests, my interest as an anthropologist is in the study of economic life among 'ordinary people' in the 'real world'. You might ask: why bother trying to study it anywhere else? And yet the discipline of economics has come to be based – to what many observers consider a remarkable extent – on the study of *unreality*, i.e. on developing and studying models that do *not* simply reflect 'how things are'. Of course, this has left the field open to some stinging criticism, not least after the 2007–2008 financial crisis, which led even economics students in the middle of their degree programmes to turn on their own teachers for (among other things) the perceived lack of realism in their work.[4] None other than the chief economist of the World Bank has subsequently attacked his fellow economists for their blind allegiance to what he calls 'post real' models and assumptions.[5]

But whether these (by now widely voiced) criticisms truly hit the mark remains a matter of debate. A helpful intervention, at least from an outsider's perspective, has recently been made by Ricardo Reis, a macro-economist (Reis 2018). He considers the state of his own subfield in relation to four very different kinds of activity: research, policy, forecasting and teaching. In doing so, he also looks at work that is being done by a sample of young macroeconomists and at articles that are being published in one of the leading (mainstream) journals – all of which he finds useful means of clarifying what the presumed crisis in economics is about. I should mention that Reis himself is critical of certain trends in his discipline. Indeed, he makes the broader point that *everything* is wrong with macroeconomics and that the task at hand is precisely to try to sort out 'flaws in our current knowledge'. But he nevertheless concludes that the public attacks have been off target, on the whole. In particular, the idea that economics has become detached from reality is one that he summarily rejects.

In support of this, he cites (among others) Arlene Wong, a 2016 PhD whose work focuses on monetary policy and consumption.[6] In Reis's summary,

Wong uses micro data to show that it is mostly young people who adjust their consumption when monetary policy changes interest rates. Younger people are more likely to obtain a new mortgage once [the] interest rate changes, either to buy a new home or to refinance an old one, and to spend the new available funds. *Her research has painstaking empirical work* that focuses on

---

[4] See Post-Crash Economics Society (2014); see also Earle, Moran and Ward-Perkins (2016).

[5] Romer (2016).

[6] At the time of writing, Wong is an assistant professor at Princeton: www.arlene-wong.com/.

the role of mortgages and their refinancing features and a model with much heterogeneity across households. (Reis 2018: 135, emphasis added)

He also cites Gregor Jarosch, a 2015 PhD whose works focus on labour market issues.[7] In Reis's summary,

Jarosch wrote a model to explain why losing your job leads to a very long-lasting decline in your lifetime wages. His hypothesis was that this is due to people climbing a ladder of jobs that are increasingly secure, so that when one has the misfortune of losing a job, this leads to a fall down the ladder and a higher likelihood of having further spells of unemployment in the future. *He used administrative social security data to find some evidence for this hypothesis.* (Reis 2018: 135, emphasis added)

Economics is a big discipline, and also a diverse one. It encompasses both academic and applied (i.e. 'real-world') branches, along with work that is more theoretically and more empirically oriented. There is microeconomics and macroeconomics, of course, but also behavioural economics (which engages directly with psychology), institutional economics (which is closer to the kinds of approach that anthropologists have an affinity for) and many other types. In any case, and further to Reis's examples, many economists – whatever their subfield or approach – *do* crunch data in an attempt to address consequential, real-world issues. Indeed, an economist might argue that they are *more* in touch with reality than your average human scientist – e.g. on the grounds that they have techniques for actually 'identifying' (in a technical sense) what has caused a given phenomenon to occur. What could be more real than that?[8]

---

[7] At the time of writing, Jarosch is an assistant professor at Princeton: https://sites.google.com/site/gregorjarosch/home.
[8] For a thought-provoking introduction to empirical economics, see Angrist and Pischke (2009). For a critical, but in most respects broadly sympathetic, discussion of the 'unreal' assumptions that rationalist/theoretical economists make, and the real-world problems this can lead to, see Schlefer (2012).

Still, economics can be described as being a *rationalist* discipline, in the end. That is, the ultimate point of the exercise – one that is in line with a long and distinguished scholarly tradition – is to figure things out *not* by simply gathering more and more facts about the world but rather through an operation of the intellect, typically in the form of mathematical modelling. To put this differently, economists (including empirical economists, who are never just 'fact collectors' per se) can be said to have intentionally, rather than inadvertently, stepped back from reality. But why? With reference to theoretically oriented (i.e. model-building) economists, Robert Solow suggests that these are people 'whose attention is riveted on a *make-believe world*, whose goal is to understand everything about that world' (Solow 1997: 69, emphasis added). He then goes on to add:

Most [of them] hope that their particular make-believe world can tell us something, although obviously not everything, about the world we actually live in. The made-up world has a disadvantage. It may be an untrustworthy guide to the real world, the way a large-scale map may not tell you that the forest it shows is infested with poison ivy. But the made-up world has an advantage, too. It is possible to understand it completely. The real world is much too complicated for that. (Solow 1997: 69)

Anthropology, by contrast, can be described as an unapologetically *empiricist* discipline. In fact, anthropologists are arguably more radically empiricist than any other group of human scientists. Even light-touch exercises in rationalism, such as the sparing use of ideal types purely for the sake of discussion, make most anthropologists very nervous, in my experience. Their aim, to borrow Solow's phrase, is to study 'the world we actually live in' – and moreover to do so in exhaustive detail, with particular attention to what it really feels like to be a person in a given setting. Far from wanting to simplify things and reduce the variables under consideration, as an economist might for the sake of modelling, they set out to capture as much real-world complexity as they possibly can.

From their starting point in this strong brand of empiricism, anthropologists have come to hold not only scientific objections to economics but also what might be called normative, moral and/or political ones. As I noted in the Preface, anthropology is today an intrinsically radical discipline. Not unrelatedly, the bulk of anthropological fieldwork over the years (almost irrespective of geographical location) has been carried out alongside ordinary people who are relatively disadvantaged in global terms, sometimes dramatically so. As you might expect, anthropologists tend to align themselves with these people, with whom their own life trajectories become entangled. Along the way, many of them have grown to suspect that economists – with their 'unreal' models and their outsized political influence – play at least some role, and possibly a major role, in creating and sustaining unfair outcomes for the kinds of people they study. To put this differently, the normative/moral/political objection of anthropologists is not so much to do with the famous disconnect between economics and reality but rather with the fact that economists sometimes help *create* bad realities. Note that this charge may be levelled at seemingly well-meaning economists such as those working for development NGOs, whose initiatives many anthropologists are highly critical of.[9]

To insert a placeholder, readers might want to think about how this normative critique of economics would look from the vantage point of an anthropologist who happened to have carried out his fieldwork in Taiwan and China – both of which have had very particular trajectories vis-à-vis the experience of global capitalism and of economic growth over the past century. In the case of China, hundreds of millions of people have been lifted out of absolute poverty since Mao's death in 1976. A good deal of suffering and exploitation accompanied this, but then again a good deal of suffering and exploitation preceded it too.

---

[9] For discussions of how economic models *create* social realities, see Mitchell (2005), MacKenzie (2006) and Weszkalnys (2011). See also Wren-Lewis (2015, 2016) for interesting thoughts on recent austerity policies in the United Kingdom and the role of economics as a discipline in relation to them.

And it is a stunning achievement. Who, or what, should be given the credit? In any event, China is not the average ethnographic case study.

Meanwhile, the anthropologists' *scientific* objection to economics rests on two interconnected points. First, they hold that economists' work ignores a crucial real-world fact: that economy is always 'embedded' in wider social, cultural and historical orders – and is therefore shaped by values, practices and institutions that vary significantly across space and time. In short, the economists' approach is flawed as a natural consequence of its ahistorical and universalistic starting point.[10] Second, economists' grasp of human agency is also flawed, according to anthropologists, ignoring as it does the social/cultural/historical environments in which (real) humans live. In particular, the notion of the 'rational utility-maximising individual' is a caricature both of what it is to be human and of how humans think.

Whatever one makes of the first critique (concerning cultural-historical variation in economic life), strong – one might say overwhelming – support for the second critique (concerning economic agency and the notion of rational choice) has come in recent years from the field of economic psychology, broadly defined to include behavioural economics and a range of other approaches.[11] A towering figure in this field, Daniel Kahneman, tells us that he first learned of the psychological assumptions of standard economics from

[10] Note that this complaint is subject to two readings. One can argue that economists' account of modern capitalism is – or at least might be – broadly correct but that it should not be transplanted to non-Western or 'traditional' societies. Or one can argue that the 'dis-embedded' approach of economists is simply wrong, including in relation to modern/Western capitalism. In other words, economic life in *all* societies (not just traditional non-capitalist ones) is embedded in wider sociocultural-historical orders, a crucial fact that is left out of mainstream economic theory. For an influential study of embeddedness in the modern West, see Granovetter (1974/1995, 1985).

[11] For the sake of simplicity, I take 'economic psychology' to include behavioural economics, experimental economics, game theory and related fields, but it should be noted that the assumptions and approaches of people working in these fields is sometimes radically different.

a report that Bruno Frey wrote on the subject in the early 1970s. Its first or second sentence stated that the agent of economic theory is rational and selfish, and that his tastes do not change. I found this list quite startling, because I had been professionally trained as a psychologist not to believe a word of it. (Kahneman 2003: 162)

Since then, he and many others have sought to develop a more credible kind of economic psychology, one that accounts in particular for the role that cognitive biases and dispositions play in human thought and behaviour.[12] While some of this work could be described as broadly rationalist in orientation – it uses models and sometimes engages directly with economic theory – much of it is empirical and draws on methods from experimental and social psychology. For example, one especially well-known finding is that (real) people appear to mind *losing* wealth, even a little bit of it, so much that they will pass up the chance to make significant *gains* in order to avoid such losses. In other words, they value what they own much more than what they don't own – one could say to an 'irrational' extent (i.e. they do not maximise utility).[13]

Building on such findings, one basic conclusion of interdisciplinary economic psychology is that a range of biases and dispositions lead humans, on average, to think and act in ways that are not built into standard economic models – but that clearly do have significant real-world consequences. Moreover, a good deal of this is predictable, in the sense that our deviations from the models are consistent (Ariely 2008). One question that follows from this conclusion is the extent to which the

[12] Kahneman (2003) is a version of his Nobel Prize lecture, which gives a concise overview of the main themes of his collaborative work with Amos Tversky (see http://nobelprize.org/nobel_prizes/economics/laureates/2002/kahneman-lecture.html). A more recent, and much more comprehensive, overview of Kahneman's work is found in the book he wrote for a general audience, *Thinking Fast and Slow* (Kahneman 2011).

[13] More specifically, as Kahneman puts it, our response to losses 'is consistently much more intense [by a ratio of about 2: 1] than the response to corresponding [i.e. monetarily equivalent] gains' (2003: 164).

relevant dispositions/behaviours, such as loss aversion broadly conceived, should be understood as outcomes of an evolutionary history in which they were selected for. Research in this direction has been pursued by neuroeconomists who, among other things, make use of data collected via brain imaging techniques (see Camerer et al. 2005, Sanfrey et al. 2006).

Needless to say, these lines of research do not thrill everyone. Some economists are having none of it, specifically on the grounds that – being committed rationalists – they never claimed to be drawing a truthful picture of reality (psychological or otherwise) in their work. As Gul and Pesendorfer drily observe, 'Populating economic models with "flesh and blood human beings" was never the objective of economists' (2008: 43). Still, the impact and influence of economic psychology in general, and of behavioural economics in particular, has grown markedly in recent years.

* * *

You might suppose that this would lead the (empiricist) anthropologists to join forces with the (experimental/data-oriented) psychologists for an all-out assault on the (rationalist) economists and their make-believe worlds. Far from it. One problem, so far as anthropology is concerned, is that much of the evidence in economic psychology comes from experiments that are designed to elicit certain types of behaviour from research participants. For example, an individual may be asked to divide some money with another (usually unknown and unseen) person, under a given set of rules. By analysing reactions to such tasks, researchers can try to understand the basic moral dispositions that people apply to economic transactions with others, and perhaps to life more generally. Are we prepared to give someone else nothing at all when the rules of a particular game make it possible for us to do so without fear of sanction? How does the level of generosity in such transactions change when punishment is added into the mix, e.g. if being too *un*generous might result in us being left with nothing at all? The issues explored in research of this kind are truly fascinating, in my view. But anthropologists are bound to be struck by the lack of ecological validity in the relevant tasks, i.e. by their tenuous (sometimes frankly non-existent) connection to ordinary human experience. Psychologists have an answer for this, of course, but it is not a trivial concern.

A closely related concern, also non-trivial, is that most such research has been carried out on a Western (or heavily Westernised) sample of the human species as a whole and can be said to be premised on Western assumptions, e.g. about money, exchange, fairness and so on. In short, economic psychologists appear to be as blind to cultural-historical variation as the economists are. An influential exception (not the only one, I should stress)[14] is found in the multi-sited experimental economics project carried out by Joseph Henrich and colleagues, most of whom come from evolutionary anthropology backgrounds. As it happens, the results of their ambitious project – in which standard economic experiments were run in a number of small-scale societies – essentially confirm what is folk knowledge in social and cultural anthropology. That is, universalist models of *homo economicus* are flawed because the thinking and behaviour of real-world agents is strongly influenced by culturally transmitted norms, values and practices (Henrich et al. 2004). Be that as it may, most social and cultural anthropologists cannot bring themselves to accept even the basic premises of this research, starting with its evolutionary framing and its experimental methodology, and prefer not to engage with it at all (for a detailed critique from an anthropological

[14] Because economic psychology is a large and very diverse field, the extent to which it 'ignores non-Western data' varies significantly depending on where one looks. In addition to the work of Henrich et al., discussed in this paragraph, some of the other recent work on the evolution of human cooperation is strongly oriented towards taking cross-cultural data of various kinds into account (e.g. see Bowles & Gintis 2011). Still, a high proportion of the data used for these purposes would, I think, be judged by many social and cultural anthropologists as superficial and lacking in ecological validity.

perspective, see Chibnik 2005, 2011). More generally, anthropologists who specialise in the study of economy largely proceed as if the neighbouring (and arguably complementary) field of economic psychology simply did not exist.

* * *

But here there is surely an irony. Indeed, I want to suggest that there are *two* ironies. As just noted, the influence of economic psychology has grown markedly in recent years – not least within mainstream economics itself, where hires of behavioural economists have become a routine occurrence. This is notwithstanding that the economic psychology research base suffers from what most anthropologists would consider a serious lack of ecological and cross-cultural validity. Meanwhile, economic anthropologists have carried on with their own (by definition ecologically and cross-culturally valid) field research. They have explored a wide range of important real-world topics in this way, such as the global economy of 'care', emerging forms of debt under neoliberalism, the socioeconomic consequences of large-scale infrastructure projects, etc. What they have basically *not* studied, however, are the psychological mechanisms that make economic life as we know it possible in the first place. Why not?

The answer rests partly in a general Durkheimian antipathy that anthropologists hold towards explaining *any* social phenomenon with reference to 'individual psychology'. (In the background of this, as I will discuss later on, one finds the rather misleading assumption that psychology as a discipline is firmly rooted in an individualist/atomist epistemology, by contrast with the relational/holist epistemology that anthropologists – also rather misleadingly – are presumed to take as their starting point.) Note that this antipathy to psychology may be especially strong in cases where a particular explanation has an evolutionary, and thus explicitly universalist, angle to it. Even when focusing on such things as emotional experience, for example, anthropologists will tend to go out of their way to frame this as a sociocultural phenomenon rather than an individual psychological and/or evolutionary phenomenon, e.g. by avoiding the word 'emotion' or by treating human feelings as cultural constructs.[15] As a consequence, they more or less rule out – to put it less charitably, manage to avoid – any serious engagement with the recent findings of psychologists.

More specifically, however, the anti-psychologism of *economic* anthropology (as opposed to the discipline's more generic antipathy) is linked to the critique of economics I have already outlined earlier. So, let me add a few more words about this by way of background. Drawing inspiration from the work of Polanyi – which had its roots in a version of Marxism (see Burawoy 2003) – anthropologists have long distinguished between two different ways of approaching economic analysis. The *formalist* approach (which holds sway in economics but is very much a minority interest among anthropologists) has the question of utility maximisation under conditions of scarcity at its core. More specifically, this approach is premised on a psychological assumption: that under conditions of scarcity humans *will* on aggregate behave as rational maximisers of utility. But here let me add an important point. Even if this rationality assumption is adopted by formalists/economists purely for the sake of model building – that is, without them claiming that it always holds at the individual level in the real world – they undoubtedly *do* believe that economic life *is* psychological. Economic agents may be rational or not, by some definition, but they are definitely thinking and making crucial choices about how best to live their lives.

By contrast, the *substantivist* approach (strictly a minority interest in economics, but truly hegemonic among anthropologists) takes the position I have outlined previously. Economic life is embedded in particular

---

[15] For example, Richard and Rudnyckyj, in speaking of 'affective economies', state that they prefer to avoid using the term 'emotion' because 'emotion as an analytical concept still bears *the spectre of a psychological individualism*' (2009: 61, emphasis added).

social, cultural and historical orders. To conceive of it as falling into a separate 'market' domain – detached from everything else, including the historically particular institutions of kinship, religion and politics that we found in actual human societies – is basically an ideological move. Further to this, substantivists argue for a radical shift of approach. The 'choices' (utility maximising or not) made by real-world economic agents are so heavily constrained by social and cultural determinants that we ought to study these determinants and forget about the choices as such (e.g. see Ferguson 1985). More specifically, we should abandon the formalists' singular focus on utility maximisation under conditions of scarcity – which, so far as anthropologists are concerned, is simply the obsession of an economic science that, moreover, helps prop up capitalism – and shift towards a broader focus on how humans collectively make a living in history.

Much has been written about the debate between formalism and substantivism, and I will not revise the arguments here.[16] However, I do want to highlight an important, in my view fatal, slippage that goes along with the rejection of formalism. It is as if the anthropologists, having (not unreasonably) rejected the idea that humans are rational maximisers of utility, have gone on to infer that economic life is therefore *not psychological*. As my opening story from Protected Mountain reminds us, however, this simply *is* a domain of life in which we learn, think, feel, calculate, judge, decide and so on. How could it be otherwise?

Moreover, the broadly Marxist-Hegelian tradition that apparently pushed economic anthropology *away* from exploring psychology

---

[16] For a useful overview, including an account of Polanyi's ongoing influence, see Hann and Hart (2011). My own position on these debates is perhaps closest to that of Granovetter. While agreeing with substantivists about the 'embeddedness' of economic life, he goes on to argue (as does the anthropologist Fredrik Barth) that an understanding of social process – anywhere – requires attention to the networks of relations within which interests, preferences, ambitions, etc., are acted upon (Granovetter 1985; see also Barth 1967). Note, however, that neither Granovetter nor Barth really take up the specifically psychological implications of this position in any detail, a point I discuss in Chapter 3.

should instead have pushed it in the opposite direction – or so I will be arguing in this book. After all, economic agency is *the* central analytical focus for Marx not only because it drives human history but also because it shapes human consciousness, the two things being mutually implicated at every step of the way. To study economy without taking psychology and human consciousness properly into account is actually un-Marxist, in my view – but this is exactly where we find ourselves today in the discipline of anthropology. That is the first irony (meaning we go to considerable lengths to elide the very thing we ought to be focusing on, in light of our own intellectual heritage). As a consequence, and here is the second irony, there is now a vast amount of data emerging from behavioural economics and other fields about the economic psychology of a purely imagined and/or experimentally constructed world, but we so far have remarkably little *ethnographic* data about the economic psychology of the world in which we actually live.

* * *

But perhaps this is putting it too strongly. In addition to conducting economic experiments in small-scale societies, the evolutionary anthropologists in the Henrich-led project cited earlier have done a good deal of ethnographic work on real-world economic psychology. Over the years, a number of social and cultural anthropologists have arguably[17] done the same thing, starting with the so-called formalists who were interested in utility, planning, etc. If I were to sum up economic anthropology today, however, I would say that it is dominated by two types of 'non-psychological substantivism'. There is a broadly materialist (i.e. more explicitly political-economy-oriented) branch – following in the footsteps of Sidney Mintz and others – that stresses power relations and focuses on patterns of exploitation, inequality and resistance. And

---

[17] I use the qualifier 'arguably' in this sentence because although the work I'm referring to does engage with economic models of utility, choice, etc., it typically does *not* engage with the specifically psychological implications of these models.

there is a more culturalist branch – following in the footsteps of Clifford Geertz and others – that stresses the meaningful or symbolic aspects of economic life, and in particular the cultural construction of value, labour, consumption, care and so on. In neither of these approaches, which may be combined in the work of individual authors, does psychology get a serious look, for the reasons I have already explained.

Of course, one can argue that a significant proportion of the published ethnography of economic life is still relevant to questions in economic psychology. The problem is that it is virtually never explicitly framed or interpreted by anthropologists in relation to such questions. Nor, for that matter, are economists, psychologists and others paying much attention to the cross-cultural evidence that is there for them to consult. As the philosopher Francesco Guala has astutely observed, *theories* about the evolution of (presumably universal) psychological dispositions have been vastly more influential for contemporary debates in economic psychology than the mass of ethnographic and historical *data* that we have about actual divergences in economic life across human societies and over time (Guala 2012).

Meanwhile, a number of anthropologists have written insightfully about economic life from the perspective of learning, skill, agency, communication, etc. Among many others, Jean Lave has studied the use of arithmetic in everyday economic activities such as shopping (1988); Edwin Hutchins has studied distributed cognition in the context of work (1995); Tim Ingold has studied economic activity as a way of being in the world (2000); and Trevor Marchand has studied skill and craft, e.g. among minaret builders (2009, 2016). The research of such scholars, however, is typically taken as a contribution to the anthropology of learning, cognition and skill, and/or to anthropological theory in general, rather than to economic anthropology as such. Their findings, however well received, have not led to any fundamental rethinking, so far as one can tell, of what economic anthropology is about. Tellingly, James Carrier's *A Handbook of Economic Anthropology* – which, at over 500 pages, covers a wide range of topics in the field – has only one short article (by Sutti Ortiz) that is explicitly psychological in orientation. Among the terms that do *not* show up at all in the book's index are learning, thinking, schooling, apprenticeship, psychology, cognition, mind and emotion (Carrier 2005). Overviews of economic anthropology (including, more recently, Hann & Hart 2011) tend not to mention psychology at all – other than in the context of criticising rational-choice theory.

* * *

This brings me to what I hope to achieve in this book. In what follows, I will be describing real-world situations of the kind that are the standard fare of empiricist economic anthropology, i.e. ordinary people going about their lives in particular cultural-historical environments. As this suggests, my approach is broadly substantivist, and it is certainly not formalist. As an anthropologist, I assume that economic life is always embedded in wider social, cultural and historical orders. Beyond this, I assume that it is built as much or more around cooperative activity with known others – kin and non-kin – as it is around competitive transactions with complete strangers in the marketplace. As would the people I met in Protected Mountain and my other fieldsites in China and Taiwan, I take it for granted that economy is ultimately an *ethical* domain, not just one of abstract costs and benefits.

Unlike most anthropologists, however, I plan to keep psychology at the centre of my ethnographic account. The people I have met during my periods of fieldwork may not be 'individual rational choosers' in any simple sense. But they certainly engage in logical deliberation about their short-term economic options (e.g. whether to take part in a potentially profitable, but also dangerous, fishing expedition) as well as in longer-term life planning (e.g. what kind of career to aim for and/or how many children to have). Over time, they become both knowledgeable and skilful in ways that impinge not only on their working lives but also on the broader activity of mastering the world they simultaneously transform as cooperative social agents. In reflecting on these and other topics, I will engage with ideas from anthropology, but also with ideas from psychology and economics.

I suppose it is inevitable, in a book such as this one, that knowledgeable readers will be surprised from time to time at what I have *not* brought into the discussion. For anthropologists, the most obvious gaps will be with respect to the specialist economic anthropology and anthropology of China and Taiwan literatures. To give one brief example, when I consider how the problem of 'fate' impinges on real-world economic agency, I will only lightly reference the (copious) anthropological writings on this topic – and actually exclude altogether many of the directly relevant China- and Taiwan-specific sources that I might have drawn on. The trade-off is that I am engaging with some non-anthropological ideas and sources, and I hope colleagues will consider this worthwhile. I should also note that when it comes to engaging with the work of psychologists (aside from leaving out many references that they might have expected me to incorporate here), I will not have any experimental data of my own to draw upon. Nor, when it comes to engaging with the discipline of economics, will I do so with reference to aggregate data or mathematical modelling of the kind that economists themselves would probably consider the whole point of the exercise. (Full disclosure: even if I wanted to do so, I do not have the technical competence.) In short, I am a classic anthropological empiricist, and this is a social anthropology book. I have evidence of the kind that comes from conducting fieldwork in particular places, at particular moments, among a small handful of people. Indeed, my core sample is vanishingly small by the standards of most other human scientists. Still, I have been carrying out fieldwork in Taiwan and China since the mid-1980s, and in a diverse mix of places, not to mention that I have supervised a large number of PhD students who have done the same in a wide range of Taiwanese and Chinese communities and on a wide range of topics. In other words, the cumulative evidence I have drawn on for this book is less anecdotal than it might at first appear.

But exactly what do I think is gained from the approach I adopt in the chapters that follow, one that is ethnographically grounded while also engaging with other disciplines that have radically different starting points? First, I believe it can be helpfully disruptive to bring ideas, theories and findings from rationalist, experimental and/or evolutionary disciplines to bear on questions in empiricist economic anthropology. Rationalism has drawbacks, of course, including the risk that we might lose touch with reality altogether. But so too does empiricism have a number of (actually very well-known) drawbacks – a fact about which many of my fellow anthropologists seem to be remarkably sanguine. Bearing this in mind, I think we should have the humility to see what can be learned from other disciplines, including those about which we have scientific and/or moral misgivings.[18]

To make it explicit, my goal is not to 'rescue' economics and psychology from anthropological critique but rather to see how these disciplines can be used to enrich anthropology, and vice versa. As part of this objective, I believe we should let go of three damaging ideas that, unfortunately, have become a kind of orthodoxy in much of contemporary anthropology: (1) the idea that rationalist modelling and/or quantification is in itself a bad thing, (2) the idea that hypothesis-driven experimentation is in itself a bad thing and (3) the idea that evolutionary theorising is in itself a bad thing. If we were to let go of these ideas, we would still be perfectly entitled to complain all we like about the work of economists and psychologists.

Speaking personally, by the way, I find that by far the most serious problem with economics today is that it is such a male-dominated discipline. This situation seems to me certain to influence, among other things, economists' ideas about what 'the economy' is and what the representative economic agent is likely to be doing.

[18] See Stafford (2011b).

Second, to reverse the equation, I also believe that it can be helpfully disruptive to bring real-world findings from anthropology to bear on questions in economics and economic psychology. As just noted, empiricism has a number of drawbacks, the most famous of which is that we might conspicuously fail to see the forest for the trees. Still, the empiricist discipline of anthropology has an important, and I would say under-acknowledged, role to play in the human sciences as a whole. Through long-term participant observation fieldwork, we engage intensively with people who would otherwise almost certainly be off the map so far as our scientific and philosophical debates are concerned. And we take the (often deep) ideas and understandings of these people with the seriousness they deserve, thus helping bring the human sciences crashing back down to earth, one could say. I should add that I'm not actually a pure romantic when it comes to anthropology as a vocation. The discipline's history, and to some extent its present, is too problematic for that. But our deceptively simple methods can be productive. To put this differently, if it is true that economists' 'make-believe worlds', and psychologists' experimental worlds can help them generate important insights – as I completely accept – so too can the anthropologists' method of immersive participation in everyday social realities help them generate important insights.

Of course, some of the findings derived in this way may seem *obvious*, simply reflecting how things are in the world. Let me give a brief illustration I will return to in Chapter 2. In the Taiwanese fishing community where I carried out my first period of extended fieldwork, many important economic decisions were taken in light of spiritual considerations. That is, people there 'obviously' did things on the basis that the gods/ancestors/spirits had told them to. Of course, unless an economist just happened to be doing a study of religion (which does happen), this is not the sort of evidence he would normally need to worry about – and, as I will explain, I do consider this a defensible position. In other words, he wouldn't think of religion as being relevant to *everything* he studies, no matter how obviously important it might seem from the vantage point of an anthropologist studying Taiwan. But the implications of religion for the field of economic psychology are a bit harder to bracket off, I want to suggest. In brief, religious and other 'apparently irrational' beliefs (to use Dan Sperber's phrase [Sperber 1985]) comprise a very particular kind of human knowledge. And when such beliefs play a role in decision making – as is certainly *often* the case in human societies, and as is arguably *always* the case in human societies – they are bound to have significant real-world consequences, including economic ones. However, just as one searches in vain for references to psychology in most contributions to economic anthropology, so one searches in vain for references to religion, and indeed to culture and history more generally, in most contributions to economic psychology (e.g. this is strikingly true of Kahneman's 2011 overview of the field). This is a curious omission of an obvious fact about the particular species we are meant to be studying.

Third, and further to the last point, the approach I advocate here can give us a better understanding of how notionally 'individual' economic psychology is, in reality, always scaffolded by a wide range of cultural-historical artefacts in our cognitive environments – e.g. by such things as religion. As I said at the outset, economic life is premised on us having a number of psychological attributes, dispositions and skills. These might be said to be products of evolution: our species has evolved to have certain ways of knowing, and reacting to, the world around us. The attributes, dispositions and skills we have could also be said to be products of individual learning: by means of trial and error, we as individuals figure out how things work in our immediate environments and what we should do in response to events. Most anthropologists would want to argue, however, that neither a *nativist* (i.e. evolution-based) account of human knowing nor a *constructivist* (i.e. individual-experience-based) account will ever be adequate, on its own. Why not? Because so much of what we think and know with regard to economy and everything else is acquired via cultural learning, i.e. through interactions with those around us and with the cultural-historical artefacts in the environments where we live. The basic point is that learning of this kind, the *cultural-historical* kind, 'scaffolds' individual cognition, enabling us to do much that we could not do, at least not so effectively, if we were to rely purely on our evolved psychology and/or our individual experiences of the world.

In the context of this book, which examines the psychology of economic agency within culturally and historically specific environments, I would highlight three features of scaffolding effects of this kind:

- They take place with respect to the *logical*, the *emotional* and the *ethical* aspects of economic agency.
- They take place with respect to *individual* processes of economic agency and also to 'distributed', i.e. joint or *collective*, ones.
- They take place with respect to *micro* and *macro* phenomena, e.g. with respect to two children reckoning prices during a sales transaction in front of a rural temple but also with respect to the shared economic history of an entire community or region.

* * *

This discussion takes us back to Protected Mountain.

One basic point that can be drawn from my opening story about the sister and brother selling bananas in front of the Temple of Learning is that the individual psychology of economic life is always embedded in, and thus a product of, collective history. This is a very anthropological point to make. However, the same point could – and I want to argue *should* – be made the other way around. That is, the history of places like Protected Mountain is, to a significant extent, a product of the (simultaneously individual and collective) economic psychology that has unfolded there. Of course, most anthropologists prefer not to see things this way. They prefer to stick with non-psychological substantivism, which has served them well, and to avoid commenting on 'mind-internal' things that they feel are beyond their remit and outside their expertise. But in doing so they miss something crucial: economic life, taken broadly to include the social and cultural institutions in which it is embedded, is important not only because it is how we get by but also because it transforms our knowledge of ourselves and the world, thus shaping what we decide to do in history. More specifically, economic agency is at the core of human *self-education*, to us gaining a sense of who we are and of our capacities as historical agents caught up in a world of shared intentions and cooperative projects. This in particular should push anthropologists to study the psychology that underpins it.

☙

TWO

Decisions

As I have explained in the Introduction, anthropologists have long rejected what they characterise as 'formalist' approaches to the study of economy. They reject in particular the notion of the individual utility-maximising choice agent on which the standard formalism of economists, so far as they understand this approach, has been premised. In his book-length treatment of the subject of choice, the anthropologist Michael Chibnik – who actually sought to apply rational-choice frameworks to fieldwork data early in his career – sets out his own version of this anthropological position in detail, providing empirical case studies to back up his points (Chibnik 2011). In brief, and this is classic substantivism, the choices that real-world economic agents make are always (inevitably) framed by a wide range of social, cultural and historical variables. Human choices are thus only 'free' in a restricted sense, i.e. because the field of choice itself is a social, cultural and historical construct. Even where choice clearly *is* being exercised in some obvious way – e.g. in one-off purchasing decisions – economic agency within human communities is vastly more complex than economists' simplifying models can ever hope to account for.

In this chapter, I am going to illustrate (yet again) some of these anthropological points by means of an extended case study from Taiwan. More specifically, I will describe the role that some *religious* beliefs and practices play when it comes to economic decision making in a Taiwanese fishing community. Life there is … complicated, as we will see. Allow me to stress up front, however, that complicated real-life stories of the kind I will tell in this chapter can never, on their own, *disprove* what rationalist economists have to say about the world. Economists know very well that life is complicated. More broadly, as Milton Friedman has explained, the criticism that a particular economic model has assumptions in it that are unreal

is largely beside the point unless supplemented by evidence that a hypothesis differing in one or another of these respects from the theory being criticized yields better predictions for as wide a range of phenomena. Yet most such criticism is not so supplemented; it is based almost entirely on supposedly directly perceived discrepancies between the 'assumptions' and the 'real world'. (Friedman 1966: 31)

Let us not imagine, then, that the dose of reality I present in this chapter is suddenly going to change how economists view things. I seriously doubt that it will. On the contrary, it will probably just remind economists why they didn't become anthropologists.

That being so, my aim here is *not* just to reiterate the standard anthropological point about the role played by social/cultural/historical variables in real-world economic agency, important though this point may be. Rather, what I will argue (and in this I differ somewhat from Chibnik[1]) is that the *anthropological* understanding of such variables will be enhanced if we consider the specifically *psychological* mechanisms through which they come both (a) to exist and (b) to matter. To put this more simply, my goal here is to psychologise the important

---

[1] As I will discuss in Chapter 3, Chibnik – who is not keen on 'culturalist' approaches in anthropology – is also sceptical about approaches that have sought to bring anthropology and psychology together in the study of economic life, and in particular he is critical of the Henrich-led project in cross-cultural experimental economics. He adopts instead what is essentially a behaviourist approach, i.e. one in which we look at aggregate behavioural outcomes rather than the psychological processes that lead up to them.

point that anthropologists have been making all along, i.e. the one about the embeddedness of economy. Further to this, my stories will be interspersed with references to recent work in interdisciplinary economic psychology. (In Chapter 4, I will turn more directly to the work of economists.)

But let me add another word by way of introduction. Although I will, in what follows, spell out some culturally specific beliefs and practices, my argument is ultimately a *universalist* one. With this in mind, please do not read this as a chapter that is about 'them' – about people in rural Taiwan who happen to be religious in their uniquely Taiwanese way – but rather as one that is about you. More specifically, my argument will be that both religion and kinship profoundly influence economic agency in *all* human societies, a fact that has major implications for how you live (and think) as well.

* * *

In the mid to late 1980s, long before my arrival in Protected Mountain (the Chinese community described at the start of the Introduction), I lived for about eighteen months in a very different kind of place: the Taiwanese fishing community of Angang.[2] I found Angang, like much of rural Taiwan at the time, to be a fascinating mix of the modern and the apparently 'traditional'. Among other things, many of the people I lived alongside there were deeply religious and (when they were not watching television and racing around on their motorbikes) invested a significant proportion of their time, energy and money in the worship of Buddhist and Daoist spirits at tradition-saturated local temples, at private spirit-medium altars and in their own homes.

---

[2] As already noted, place and personal names in this book have been changed in order to protect the privacy of my informants. In some cases, I have changed other details about my informants (occupation, family size, etc.), but not in ways that affect the substantive points being made in my discussion. More details about life in Angang can be found in Stafford (1995).

After a few months of living in Angang, I became friendly with two families who shared both a sibling connection and a religious one. The head of the first family was Mr Su. He was a fisherman but also a local spirit medium (or *jitong*, 'divining child'), which meant that the gods regularly took over his body and spoke through him to local families, as they had through his father when the elder Su was still alive. The second family was headed by another fisherman, Mr Lin. His wife was Mr Su's sister, and she too was a local spirit medium. But whereas Mr Su spoke primarily for one of the warlike Wang Ye gods, his sister, Mrs Lin, spoke for nurturing female deities, including Mazu, who is famous and much loved for her role in protecting fishermen and their families from harm.

Like most people in Angang, the Su and Lin families engaged in a number of sideline economic activities in order to supplement the men's fishing income, but this was especially noticeable in the case of the Lins. They farmed very small plots of land belonging to themselves and others, they raised deer in a shed next to their house and marketed the antlers for use in medicinal wine, they sold religious paraphernalia to devotees of Mrs Lin's spirit-medium altar and they cultivated a relationship with a local construction boss who hired them for occasional waged labour. As the anthropologist Fei Xiaotong noted long ago with respect to silkworm farming in Jiangsu, China, the extra income from such sideline activities provides crucial insurance against the risks faced by rural households (Fei 1939), and the same remains broadly true today. This strategy may be especially important for those who depend on fishing, which provides a notoriously volatile livelihood.

In fact, during the time I lived in Angang, the fishing economy – based primarily around small boats with crews of two to six men – was under serious threat, as a consequence of industrial-scale over-fishing in the Pacific. The short trips made by local boats into nearby waters were increasingly unproductive. However, there was also the option of sailing, illegally, via the Luzon Strait to the Philippines. The catches were typically much better there than in the waters around Taiwan, I was told, and quite a bit of money could be made in a short time. On one ten-day trip, for instance, Mr Lin told me that he earned about US$35 per day, which compared very well with the US$10 per day he could make, back then, working on construction projects. And it compared extremely well with making nothing at all while sitting around the house chatting with friends or even losing money through gambling – bearing in mind that there were many weeks of the year when fishermen in Angang could not work at all due to seasonal constraints or other factors.

Still, a trip to the Philippines carried very significant risks, including the possibility of being caught up in violent weather, of being arrested for illegal fishing or even of being attacked by pirates while on the sea. People had to decide if the potential rewards merited taking these risks.

* * *

One afternoon when some of the local fishing boats *had* gone to the Philippines, I came upon Mr Su and his wife sitting at home playing with their granddaughter. Clearly, he was going nowhere. He told me, in passing, that it used to be remarkably easy to fish right there around Angang:

You could even use nets off the shore, and as soon as you put them out you had fish. But it's gotten worse because people are clever now. They have all these techniques, and all the fish have been caught. Still, I don't dare go to the Philippines – I might get arrested.

At this point his wife intervened. 'Hah!' she exclaimed, 'I'm the one who told him not to go. We have enough to eat three meals a day; we don't need more than that.'

A couple of days later, I went to the house of Mr Su's brother-in-law, Mr Lin, knowing that he and his fellow crewmembers *had*, for their part, gone to the Philippines. I came upon his wife standing in the small vegetable plot in front of the house, wincing in pain from a gut problem that everyone said was linked to her role as a spirit medium. As I arrived, she straightened up and looked angrily at the sea. Although in my experience she was a strong woman, I could see that on this day Mrs Lin was truly anxious about her husband's safety – and the weather reports for the Luzon Strait were ominous. To my surprise, she burst into tears, leading her teenage daughter, who was standing nearby, to mockingly say, 'Ah, now you're *crying*!' (In Angang, there was a generalised culture of encouraging toughness, including within notably warm and loving families.)

Soon after she started crying, a local, unofficial Daoist priest (a close relative) arrived at her home and began preparing for a spirit-medium session involving Mrs Lin and the 'bright spirits' for whom she spoke. She came inside and stood near the altar. Her body convulsed, and in the voice of a goddess, she dealt quickly, even perfunctorily, with a few passing matters: a child's poor health, the selection of lottery numbers for a client, the potentially dangerous movements of a restless spirit around Angang. So far as I could tell, nothing was said on this occasion about her husband and his fellow crewmembers. As she went on, several friends, regulars at her altar, showed up to listen. And then, once Mrs Lin had finished talking – and had slumped down in a side room in apparent discomfort – these friends simply helped themselves to food and drink from her house in the highly familiar manner typical of social life in Angang. Nobody humoured or indulged her in any obvious way. But there's an important point about this nonchalant behaviour: both Mrs Lin and her friends would have known that the friends' display of almost aggressive familiarity was evidence that they would all be there to help her and her children if it were to become necessary later on, e.g. if her husband should come to harm while out fishing…

* * *

An obvious question that follows is why Mr Lin and his fellow crewmembers went to the Philippines to fish, whereas Mr Su and his fellow crewmembers did not. And I presume that most anthropologists can easily guess, at this point, where the story is headed. In the real world, even a straight yes/no decision about something as simple as a single fishing trip turns out to be incredibly complicated, not least because a wide range of social and cultural particularities can have a bearing on the outcome. As I have just been suggesting, for example, a risk-mitigating factor in the particular case of Mr and Mrs Lin *might* have been the availability to her of a support network of close friends – who communicate this support in a culturally specific way via indirect behavioural cues that might not be obvious at all to outsiders. Note, however, that the underlying logic of both decisions in this case was arguably quite straightforward. Perhaps more importantly, most people in Angang – and I would say across rural Taiwan and China – would quickly grasp this logic, because it is consistent with a widely held folk model of why families do what they do.

Let me pause here to explain: in this book, I will primarily use the word 'logical' and variations on it in preference to the word 'rational' and variations on it when referring to the everyday thinking of my research interlocutors. I do so partly because notions of rationality and irrationality have become so loaded in human science debates about economy. As Daniel Kahneman observes, 'irrational is a strong word', and to simply invoke it (and/or 'rational') can be quite problematic (2011: 411). Certainly, the people I've met during fieldwork in Taiwan and China *reason* a great deal about the economy; but whether the outcomes of this are rational by any formal definition is another thing, and that is not my main concern anyway. Of course, many readers might feel that the word 'logical' – which I use here in a folk rather than a technical sense – is equally problematic. Moreover, there is a complex story to be told about the relationship between 'logic' and 'reason' as categories in the pre-history of cognitive science (Mercier and Sperber 2017: 34–48). Still, I hope that my usage will at least flag the fact that I am not making any rationality – or irrationality – assumptions per se when it comes to my understanding of economic agency in the real world. I also hope that doing so helps capture the fact that the people I've met, when they are considering alternative courses of action in their lives, *do* routinely proceed in a deliberative 'if *x* then *y*' manner, i.e. in an explicitly *logical* manner. Many anthropologists, in their eagerness not to make rationality assumptions in relation to the people they study, overlook this incredibly important fact.

So, what is the logic in these two cases? Briefly, both the Lins and the Sus have children. In line with the traditional view, their hope is that these children will help them in old age – or at least be hypothetically willing to, even if it turns out that help isn't needed in the end. However, there's an important difference between the two families: the Sus and their children are older than the Lins and their children. At the time of my fieldwork, the Lins' son and daughter were still in school, did not have jobs, and were not married. As a result, they were not yet making a financial contribution to their family, and it was hard to guess what might happen to them later on in terms of occupation, marriage or residence. By contrast, the Su daughters were already employed elsewhere in Taiwan. More importantly, their son held a secure, if low-paid, job right there in Angang and lived at home with his parents and his wife, who was originally from Taipei. Crucially, then, the very considerable marriage costs for the Su's son had been met, he was already employed and contributing to the family finances, and he had agreed to live in or near his parents' home and eventually look after them. Furthermore, he and his wife had already produced one grandchild at the time of my fieldwork.

In terms of the standard set of life concerns for rural Taiwanese families, this meant that the Sus – compared to the Lins – were in good shape. When Mrs Su said that her husband did not need to go to the Philippines because they had enough to 'eat three meals a day', she might have added that their affairs were more generally in order. This probably made it easier for her to convince Mr Su to stay at home, just as – conversely – the Lins' situation may have made it easier for Mr Lin to persuade his wife that risks needed to be taken, at least for the time being. It may also help explain why the Lins, more so than the Sus, took up sideline activities in order to generate extra income. They basically needed it more. Under these circumstances, then, the decisions and actions of the Su and Lin families would be seen by their neighbours and friends as quite logical or reasonable (*you daoli*), even if not everybody would agree with what they did.

Indeed, my assumption is that the overall pattern of such decisions and actions in Taiwan – which, after all, is a very market-oriented, even market-obsessed, society – is equally logical in terms of its underlying basis. At the time of my fieldwork, fishermen in Angang were attracted by the high returns from long-distance fishing trips but naturally worried about the considerable risks too. All other things being equal, if the returns had risen dramatically, the number of fishermen prepared to confront the risks would surely have gone up as well (presumably starting with those who had reason to be the least risk-averse). If, by contrast, the risks had risen sharply – e.g. because of a spike in pirate attacks that became prolonged – it seems to me likely that few, if any, of them would have made trips to the Philippines any more (presumably starting with those who had reason to be the most risk-averse). Indeed, what seems to have happened over the years since my fieldwork in Angang is precisely that most Taiwanese people have opted out of small-boat, long-distance fishing altogether, i.e. because the reward-to-risk ratio is now considered so unfavourable compared with the risk of other ways of making a living.[3]

* * *

This is the sort of collective outcome that an economist might find interesting. The details could be debated, of course, and the discussion could go in many directions. What role might (potentially volatile) insurance

[3] The long-distance fishing industry in Taiwan has been both heavily regulated and relatively high risk, not least because of the continued threat of kidnapping by pirates. But one significant change over time has been a shift towards foreign crews (especially from Indonesia) working on boats under the management of a Taiwanese captain, as fewer Taiwanese are prepared to take up the profession (see Shih et al. 2010, Ting et al. 2012).

costs play in all of this? How might broad economic trends, such as Taiwan's growth trajectory in relation to China's, affect investment in various sectors that impinge on the local economy, including the fishing sector on which these families depend? How might wage 'stickiness' in the wider labour market affect the ability or willingness of fishermen from Angang to move into different, perhaps safer, occupations? In any case, it does seem that the market as a whole has a logic and a collective direction of travel that is relatively non-mysterious. An economist could figure it out.

If we're interested in actual processes of everyday decision making, however, things aren't so straightforward (and an economist might not be so helpful). One major complication is that fishing is a joint activity, not an individual one. Mr Lin and Mr Su work on boats with other crewmembers, and these men – whose family circumstances may vary a lot – need to confer with each other about their plans. Meanwhile, their wives, their parents (almost all of whom live locally and come from fishing backgrounds), their friends and even their children may express strong opinions about things, so that in the end the number of people involved in debating a single potential trip to the Philippines is likely to be large. One can imagine a network of individuals spreading out from each boat along which a number of informational and emotional transactions occur.

But more is at stake here than complex informational and emotional transactions between individuals within an expanding decision-making network. For a crucial role is also played in such transactions, and in local decision-making processes as a whole, by a wide range of cultural-historical artefacts – ideas, objects, practices, routines, institutions, etc. – that are to be found in the cognitive environment of Angang. To explain, the use of the term *artefact* indicates that these ideas, objects, practices, etc., are not just naturally occurring phenomena but rather historical realisations of human thought, communication and action. A Taiwanese fishing boat is an artefact, in this sense, but so too are religious rituals, the way in which fish-selling transactions happen to be handled at Angang's harbour, the Confucian notion of filial obedience and so on. Moreover, the continued real-world relevance of these artefacts (be it in Angang or elsewhere) depends on ongoing processes of interaction and cultural transmission between thinking agents. Labelling these highly diverse phenomena *cultural-historical* helps remind us not only that they vary culturally (e.g. that Taiwanese economic practices may be different from those to be found in other places, such as Japan), but also that they vary historically (e.g. that Taiwanese economic practices may look different before, during and after the Japanese colonial era).

But let me give a concrete example of one artefact that is directly relevant to the case I'm describing. Mrs Su's ability to stop her husband from going to the Philippines rests in part on a local norm/artefact related to gender: women in Angang often have the final say when it comes to their husbands' plans. Notwithstanding the patriarchal orientation of traditional Chinese culture, Angang is actually a place where, in fact, many women have a good deal of power.[4] So it isn't simply that this one particular woman, individually, is able to control her husband's decisions to some extent, but also that this widely distributed norm/artefact puts her in a stronger position to do so. Meanwhile, the understanding/artefact that 'a fisherman, once he has a grandchild, has less need to take risks' clearly depends on a particular way of seeing the world. Such an understanding isn't unique to Taiwan, obviously, but at the time of my fieldwork it did come in a culturally and historically particular form there (I will come back to this point near the end of the chapter).

As Ed Hutchins has explained in his important discussion of 'cognition in the wild' (1995), artefacts of these kinds really *do* things when

---

[4] For a more detailed discussion of this, and of the 'matriarchal' orientation of Chinese culture, see Stafford (2008a). Yunxiang Yan has also written very interestingly about the extent to which women participate in and/or control household decisions in north China, something he attributes to changing gender relations and the rise of women's power (Yan 2003).

it comes to human activity. They motivate us to act in particular directions (e.g. towards greater risk-taking or not), they enable and shape communication between individual agents within networks of decision making and action (e.g. making it more or less likely that a woman will speak up to her husband) and in some cases they effectively take decisions completely out of our hands – as happens in a coin toss.

* * *

Now, it might be felt that by bringing artefacts into our discussion of economic decision making in Angang we have moved things in a notably anthropology-friendly direction. The focus on artefacts shifts our attention away from 'mind-internal' individual psychology and towards what might be called 'mind-external' (for which read social and cultural) factors instead. In short, this move reduces the importance of what is going on inside of people's heads. However, the key point to keep bearing in mind – meaning, throughout the whole book – is that such artefacts are *themselves* psychological phenomena. That is, not only do they produce cognitive effects (i.e. they influence how we think), but they themselves are outcomes of cognitive processes (i.e. their shape and content is a consequence of, among other things, how humans think as well as the particulars of learning and cultural transmission in our species). In any case, a central goal of my book, as I explained from the outset, is to *not* sidestep the psychological dimensions of economic agency as anthropologists have typically done. In what follows, I therefore will be focusing in more detail on some notionally 'mind-internal' phenomena – beliefs and emotions – that turn out to matter a lot for economic decision making in Angang. More to the point, I want to examine the *relationship* between these mind-internal phenomena and the cultural-historical artefacts that are embedded in the cognitive environments where our real-world decision makers live.

But here let me add a few general comments about recent research in the psychology of decision making before returning to this case study.

This is a huge and highly diverse field, but one central focus has been on unpacking the relationship between *automatic* and *controlled* psychological processes that bear on decision-making processes (for an overview, see Camerer et al. 2005). Putting this in more accessible language for a general readership, Kahneman (2011) draws an ideal-type contrast between what he refers to as 'fast' and 'slow' thinking. When faced with a decision – e.g. concerning a risky but potentially profitable fishing trip – an individual might invest a good deal of time and trouble in thinking things through, weighing up the costs and benefits in a logical way. However, even during 'slow' (controlled, effortful) deliberation of this kind, other things are going on. In brief, we react to our circumstances via 'fast' processes that may profoundly shape our view of what can and should be done in response to them. Obviously, it is part of our folk psychology to say that gut reactions matter in life. But the research highlights something more fundamental than this: that psychological processes we can't access at all and which, crucially, might also not be susceptible to cultural learning – including instantaneous risk calculations, feelings/emotions below the level of explicit awareness, and unconscious biases that influence information processing – may guide, even determine, our decisions and subsequent actions. For example, we might rapidly gauge the probability of a given thing happening. The evidence suggests that in doing so, however, we're inclined both to (intuitively) overestimate the probability of unlikely events occurring and to (intuitively) overweigh the potential for such events in our deliberations (Kahneman 2011: 324).

As noted in the Introduction, findings of this sort have undermined the rational choice model of human decision making, at least to some extent, thus raising important questions for economists. But the findings also raise important questions for anthropologists. Among other things, if some of the most important elements in human decision making are unconscious, as Kahneman and others appear to have shown, can our fieldwork interlocutors ever give us reliable accounts of why they do what they do – and more generally of the thinking behind their (prospective or completed) actions in the world?

Still, it is a very common human activity – precisely – to explain and defend our decisions and actions. Notably, both Mr and Mrs Su were quick to justify the fact that he did not go to the Philippines: he told me it was the fear of arrest; she told me it was because she told him not to go. Further to this example, it has been proposed that human reasoning evolved *not* for the purpose of helping us decide, as such – and the evidence suggests that we are not, on the whole, very good decision makers – but rather for the purpose of … handling social relations. More specifically, this skill evolved to help us argue with and persuade those around us of various things, and to help us evaluate the arguments of others. These are crucial abilities in an intrinsically social species. One piece of evidence for the 'argumentative theory of reason' (Mercier & Sperber 2011, 2017) is that people routinely make what are known as reason-based choices (e.g. see Shafir 1993). That is, their decisions are based not on weighing up the costs and benefits of particular actions in a logical way but rather on the availability in the social environment of plausible explanations for these actions (by definition, ones that have a chance of resonating with the intended audience).

I suppose that some readers may feel that putting these two points together – (a) about fast/automatic decision making (which implies that our decisions are effectively out of our control, not to mention that we bring a number of cognitive biases into the mix) and (b) about argumentative reason (which implies that we care more about self-justification than about taking good decisions) – leads overall to quite a negative picture of the cognitive abilities of humans. As the illustration from Angang reminds us, however, we rarely take decisions in isolation from the world around us. Indeed, the argumentative theory of reason highlights precisely the extent to which reasoning is a social act. Furthermore, the psychologist Gerd Gigerenzer advocates for an approach to decision making that starts from the natural and social environments in which humans live.[5] In such environments, it may, among other things, be wise to make reason-based choices, because this can turn out to be a good heuristic. Starting from a different angle, the cognitive anthropologist Naomi Quinn (1978) also concludes that everyday folk economic reasoning can, in fact, be highly effective. Contrary to the assumptions built into some models of economic decision making, she found that the Mfantse fish sellers she studied were not doing anything like probabilistic reasoning in their (individual) heads when it came to marketing activities. On the contrary, they just let easily available heuristics in the social environment guide their approach to daily market conditions.

In terms of my own discussion, the key point is that individual thought – the notionally mind-internal part of this, such as the 'logical' consideration of alternatives by individuals – is always going to be scaffolded by the cultural-historical artefacts in our cognitive environments, as well as by wider patterns of social relations. Indeed, anthropological work that relates in some way to decision making – e.g. by Ferguson (1985), Ortiz (2005) and Chibnik (2011) – has repeatedly underlined this fact, while unfortunately leaving out the specifically psychological part of the equation, in most cases. Of course, the underlying message from the substantivists/anthropologists is surely correct: that there is no pure category of economy – i.e. nothing disconnected from every other aspect of our life experience – and by extension no such thing as a purely *individual* agent. Moreover, as noted, anthropologists hold that what is interesting in relation to all of this is neither the psychology nor the culture of decision making per se, but rather the broader political-economic environment in which humans come to have, and imagine, certain possibilities in

---

[5] See Gigerenzer (2000, 2007, 2008). Gigerenzer is a leading critic of the 'cognitive-illusions' orientation of much of the behavioural economics research, including that carried out by Kahneman and Tversky. In simple terms, where other psychologists see us being technically irrational economic agents, Gigerenzer sees us using heuristics that make a lot of sense, given the actual environments in which we live.

their lives. Having said this, if there were no individuals with minds, all the culture and history and politics in the world couldn't make economic life as we know it unfold.

* * *

Let us go back to Angang. A striking feature of life there is not only that there are many spirit mediums about but also that people use these mediums to ask the gods for advice about more or less everything. Such advice is regularly cited as the *reason* that something has been done (or not). Indeed, even trivial decisions, such as whether or not to make a two-minute motorbike ride to the next village, may be put to the gods. This is typically done by dropping divination blocks in a heads-or-tails fashion before an altar or, for more important matters, approaching gods directly via spirit mediums – of whom, as noted, there are many scattered throughout the countryside. Certainly, the relatively important question of going, or not, to the Philippines would be put before different gods by the men on a given boat, and in some cases by members of their families acting on their own initiative at various altars.

A great deal could be said about this complex process and how it all fits together, but here I simply focus on one piece of the puzzle: a single norm/artefact of mediumship.[6] In the case I've outlined earlier in this chapter, the fact that Mr Su and Mrs Lin were themselves mediums (i.e. in addition to being a fisherman and the wife of a fisherman, respectively) set up an interesting dynamic. As I came to understand things, Mr Su would have liked to have gone to the Philippines but was stopped by his wife, whereas Mrs Lin would have liked to have stopped her husband going, and yet he went. This raises the question of why, as mediums, they did not just enlist the help of their respective gods – who have considerable power to adjudicate local issues – in an attempt to achieve their opposite ends.

[6] For detailed accounts of Chinese divination and of spirit mediums, see Elliott (1955), Jordan (1972), Jordan and Overmyer (1986) and Wolf (1990).

As you might expect, the question of whether a spirit medium *can* influence things in this way is not an easy one to answer. The standard line among believers in Angang and elsewhere in Taiwan would be that if someone is truly possessed, then he or she has absolutely no control whatever of the process; the god controls the process. However, I'm confident that most people (including fervent believers, and also the mediums themselves) take a much subtler view of how things really work in practice. They adopt a 'what if' stance towards mediumship – that is, one that assumes that mediums might, after all, be able to control things to some extent – and indeed medium sessions are centrally about *proving* to audiences that a performance is genuinely controlled by the gods.

Note that anthropologists are not generally in the business of doubting the religious beliefs of those they study or calling their religious practices into question. They want to understand what religion means and does for these people, not whether it is 'true'; actually, for anthropologists the latter is quite a boring question. Still, it is common around the world to find that religious people *themselves* have a lot to say about the truth or verifiability of religious belief and practice, and in the example I am describing, that is definitively the case. As a result, while anthropologists wouldn't normally ask, 'Do these people really believe in the gods?' they have extensively explored the nature of religious conviction, as I will now discuss.

In any case, *if* the gods for whom Mrs Lin spoke had indicated in a public way that a journey to the Philippines would be dangerous and should be avoided, this information would have been taken seriously. And *if* the gods for whom Mr Su spoke had indicated in a public way that a journey to the Philippines would be safe and lucrative, this information would have been taken seriously as well. That neither of these things happened – regardless of any control we think the mediums might have over the process – relates to a norm, a cultural-historical artefact, that strongly shapes spirit-medium activities in Angang. Briefly, mediums, when possessed, do not say or do things that might be construed as self-interested. If anything, what they say/do is likely to *contradict* the stated opinions or preferences of their 'real' (meaning non-possessed) selves, and may even damage their interests in some way. So, in relation to a proposed fishing trip, a typical pattern would be for the god to oppose it if his or her medium had just supported it beforehand (i.e. when not possessed), and vice versa.[7]

***

Now, I appreciate that some readers may doubt whether this ethnographic detail can really matter so much for economic life in Angang. (As I mentioned earlier, an economist might take all of this as an object lesson in why not to become an anthropologist.) After all, the cultural-historical artefact in question is a negative rather than a positive one, i.e. it is about what *can't* be done by a spirit medium to influence a decision. Moreover, the artefacts relevant to decisions about fishing trips in Angang include not only norms of spirit mediumship but also – and arguably much more pertinently – such things as the aggregate professional expertise of local fishermen, national and international laws that regulate fishing activity and technological developments that have decreased the risk of long-distance fishing trips. Still, my point is that if the norm/artefact about mediums not helping themselves did not exist, the decisions taken by the Su and Lin families in this particular

---

[7] For the sake of ethnographic completeness, let me add that there are sometimes mechanisms in place to limit the control of mediums over the substantive content of sessions, the most important being the use of 'interpreters' and priests who explain to devotees what a god, via the medium, wishes to communicate. However, in the case of Angang, most mediums, including Mr Su and Mrs Lin, speak directly and clearly to their clients, without need for interpretation. I might also add that mediums and their families are, in fact, free to approach all the gods they like for help and advice, e.g. at the altars of other mediums, and also that – so long as they are not possessed – they can say and do whatever they like in private or public in order to try to get their way. But what is not thought acceptable is for possession episodes to lead to (recognisably) self-interested outcomes. Indeed, the mediums I knew routinely complained that the gods they spoke for never helped them resolve their own difficulties with money, health, relationships or anything else.

case might well have been reversed – which illustrates that cultural-historical artefacts *do* shape decision outcomes, and sometimes in non-obvious ways.

Of course, an economist might point out, in response to this argument, that if the two decisions in this case *were* reversed, they would then simply *cancel each other out*. In other words, the 'change' would have no impact whatever at the aggregate level. As this illustrates, for an economist who is professionally interested in aggregates, it is actually very misleading to focus attention – as anthropologists do as a matter of routine – on variables that have a statistically trivial (even non-existent) impact on the wider economy. From the point of view of anthropologists, however, the small details that surround personal life trajectories – including the precise mechanics of receiving advice from the gods – do matter. Moreover, the artefact I am drawing attention to in this particular case is linked to issues that are, in fact, at the very heart of religious life and thus of sociality more generally in Angang. This is far from being an exotic side issue or an obscure ethnographic detail.

So here let me pose some broader questions. Do people in Angang truly believe that important economic decisions must be left to the gods? Do they feel obliged to do as the gods say (via spirit mediums)? The simple answer to these questions is yes: the majority of people in Angang are devout, so far as one can tell, and they listen carefully to divine advice, when it comes to them. During my fieldwork, for example, a woman I knew put a very important decision related to the sale of family land before the gods, and the advice received in this way was scrupulously followed. But religious belief and conviction are complex phenomena, and anthropologists have long debated how best to understand them.[8] Here I briefly cite three relatively recent (and psychology-oriented) contributions to this classic debate.

---

[8] For discussions of belief specifically relevant to China and to mediumship see Elliott (1955): 162–4 and Jordan and Overmyer (1986): 267–88. Among the many anthropological discussions of belief and doubt, two recent contributions are Pelkmans (2013, 2017).

First, Dan Sperber has suggested that 'apparently irrational beliefs' about such things as gods, spirit mediums, etc., need to be understood as special kinds of beliefs. In brief, they are representational (as opposed to factual) ones that have a semi-propositional (as opposed to propositional) content. To put this more simply, such beliefs can be said to be 'half understood'[9] in a very real sense, and their internal/external consistency is ultimately beyond knowing (Sperber 1985; see also Sperber 1997, 2009). So a fisherman in Angang may say, and truly mean it, that (a) 'the goddess will protect me from harm'. However, this is not the same kind of thing as him saying that (b) 'bad weather poses a threat to the safety of my fishing boat'. Obviously, both (a) and (b) might be relevant to a particular decision. But we should not treat them as equivalent, and nor (according to Sperber) are they equivalent for our fisherman, in cognitive terms. Believing that 'I should not go to the Philippines because the goddess told me not to' is a different kind of thing from believing that 'I should not make this fishing trip because the weather forecast is ominous'.

Second, Rita Astuti has shown that what people believe – in the case of her research, what people in rural Madagascar believe about the afterlife – may vary with context and situational priming (Astuti 2007). She finds that her Vezo interlocutors speak of life both as being terminated by death and as *not* being terminated by death. In brief, if primed with notions of ancestors and ancestral tombs, they are more likely to express/manifest a belief in life continuing after death, in spite of appearing to contradict this belief under different conditions. Astuti's findings have a number of implications, but for the case I'm considering, the key implication is this: that the relevance of religious beliefs for decisions may depend on the extent to which they have been primed

[9] This is not meant by Sperber in a derogatory sense. As he explains, the content of such beliefs 'is not just vague; it is mysterious to the believers themselves and open to an endless variety of exegeses. These are what I have called semi-propositional or half-understood beliefs' (Sperber 1985).

(or not) at given points during a decision-making process. This means we can't assume that the belief that 'the goddess will protect me from harm' is one that fishermen simply *have*, in all contexts, and apply with equal weight no matter what they are doing.

Meanwhile, further to what I have said previously, devotees in Angang must deal with another, in some ways more pressing, problem of belief: is a given medium actually genuine? As Maurice Bloch and others have observed, much of what we think about such things as gods – and by extension those who give us access to them – is taken on trust. That is, we often simply defer to the older and/or more knowledgeable people around us (Bloch 2005). This does not mean, however, that we just accept everything we are told. On the contrary, humans (including young children) seem very aware of the possibility of being misled (Harris 2012). As part of this, we are attuned to what others think and more specifically to what their *intentions* (good or bad) might be. Moreover, we rely – in religious life and elsewhere – on a range of mechanisms that are specifically dedicated to 'epistemic vigilance', i.e. to assessing the trustworthiness of others and what we learn from them (see Sperber et al. 2010).

In the case of spirit mediums, the main worry is that they might (fraudulently) manipulate what takes place during possession episodes. In order to defend against this possibility – which is conflated with the possibility that ghosts and demons could be involved in medium practices in some way – the wider community goes through a process of affirming that a given medium is in fact reliable (for detailed accounts, see Jordan 1972, Wolf 1990). Even once this has been accomplished, however, the mediums continue to work in the face of a good deal of scepticism, and this is where the norm about them not acting self-interestedly could be said to come into play. This particular norm is, in effect, a cultural-historical response (one of many in religious life) to the *psychological tendency* of humans to worry about the potentially bad intentions of others. As a result, the artefact itself does some psychological work:

- it nudges individuals to not think of (already socially pre-approved) mediums as self-interested agents,
- which could make them a bit more inclined to trust in possession episodes,
- and therefore a bit more inclined to accept advice from the gods (i.e. notwithstanding the semi propositional and situational nature of their belief in these gods),
- and, finally, to apply this advice when deciding what to do.[10]

In sum, then, this 'mind-external' cultural-historical artefact is inextricably tied to 'mind-internal' processes: it is both a product of how humans characteristically think *and* a source of ongoing cognitive effects.

* * *

As it happens, though, the question of manipulating divination results cuts in various directions. Individual worshippers, when using divination blocks in front of the gods (as a way of seeking answers from them without going through a medium), *themselves* sometimes alter the rules and/or the formulation of questions as they go along if they are unhappy with the outcomes. They may change to the 'best out of three', for example, rather than taking the answer they receive on a first drop of the blocks. And there are other, less direct, means of influencing what transpires during divination. As I've already explained, the wider community has to affirm that a given medium is genuine. To some extent, this is about ensuring that the medium will not transmit too many wrong answers or too much bad advice – as this would be understood in the court of public opinion. In other words, this is about socialising (and thus constraining) the divination process as a whole. In addition, there

---

[10] Looking at this from the outside, the artefact I'm describing here may seem rather obvious: doesn't everyone just see through it? But in the context of actual spirit-possession practices, which may be compelling at many levels (not least performatively), it adds to the general air of credibility.

is at least implicit pressure on spirit mediums to come up with answers their clients are looking for *and/or* to provide them with answers that are vague enough to be open to potentially favourable interpretation. A medium who worked too strongly against the wishes of those visiting his or her altar (i.e. the general public) would presumably run out of clients. The truth of mediumship, in short, is complicated.

But what about the mediums themselves: what do they believe, and how is *their* decision making influenced by religious and other interventions? Here I will not provide a detailed analysis of the lives, motivations, etc., of Mr Su and Mrs Lin.[11] To put it simply, however, I have no reason to doubt (having spent a good deal of time with them during fieldwork) that their religious beliefs are deeply and sincerely held. More specifically, my assumption is that the *basic* problems of belief they confront in the course of life are exactly the same as those confronted by everybody else. That is – and in the senses outlined earlier – their religious beliefs are (a) semi-propositional, (b) situationally variable and (c) framed by processes of deferring to, but also worrying about the intentions of, others. Crucially, the socially sanctioned roles of Mr Su and Mrs Lin as spirit mediums have not just come out of the blue. Their father, now deceased, was a highly respected – actually, beloved – medium in the local community, and the entire process of them following in his footsteps has been a communal as much as an individual one. The ultimate truth of what they do and believe now is inextricably linked to this fact, for them as for everyone else around them in Angang.

This situation relates, in turn, to a more general sense in which religion in Angang shapes economic decisions and economic agency. As anthropologists (in line with Durkheimian functionalism) routinely observe, religion is a means through which the social itself is constituted. Religious practice may reinforce solidarities inside and outside

---

[11] The psychology of spirit possession and of mediumship as a life calling is highly complex, as anthropologists have often discussed. Among others, see Obeyesekere's classic book-length account of one medium in Sri Lanka (Obeyesekere 1984).

of families and these, in turn, factor very heavily in life plans. Of course, the Marxist critique of this view, which I will come back to later on, is that religion is actually ideological; that is, what religion does, in fact, is to blind people to the truth about the circumstances in which they live. (Note that this, too, is a *psychological* argument.) Nevertheless, the Durkheimian account of religion is one that undoubtedly helps explain what it is to be religious, for many humans, and why they accept that religion really matters. As noted previously, Mrs Lin is surrounded by friends and devotees who are basically *overly* familiar with her – a sign they will help her and her children in the future, if this should turn out to be needed. She believes that 'the gods will protect my husband from harm', but she also knows that 'my friends (fellow believers) will be there for me if the worst happens to my husband'. A non-believer might conclude that Mrs Lin's faith in the gods, and in her ability to speak for them, is irrational superstition (*mixin*), whereas her faith in the value of the social is highly rational. But the Durkheimian point is precisely that the latter is totally dependent on the former. By extension, the holding of religious beliefs is intrinsically linked to the intense emotions of collective life within families and beyond – an issue to which I now turn.

* * *

On the day I stopped by Mrs Lin's house, she burst into tears while staring at the sea – clearly worried that something terrible might happen to her husband. When it comes to decisions about fishing trips, anxieties of this kind obviously matter, but where do they come from? That we should fear the loss of those we love and depend on seems self-evident. According to attachment theory, to be anxious about separation, abandonment and loss is, indeed, natural for humans everywhere – an *evolved* tendency, as John Bowlby had it, and one that is conflated with the emotions we feel about prospective or real experiences of loss and bereavement in the course of life (Bowlby 1980; for a recent anthropological discussion and critique from a cross-cultural perspective, see Quinn & Mageo 2013). A less obvious emotion might also be relevant in this particular case: the fear of deep water and, by extension, a particular dread of death by drowning. This, it has been argued, is another 'evolutionary-relevant' emotion felt by humans, one designed to hold us back (on average) from particular kinds of risk-taking (see Poulton & Menzies 2002). To return to Kahneman's notion of fast thinking, these are the kinds of intuitive orientations (fear of abandonment, fear of drowning) that might be cognised before they are recognisably felt, and that could influence decision making about fishing trips in some way – not to mention that, as noted, we have a general bias to overestimate the likelihood of unlikely events taking place.

Note, however, that in Angang a person's *conscious* view of both things – that is, of both separation and drowning – will be significantly influenced by cultural learning. More specifically, it will be influenced through steady engagement, from childhood, with a range of cultural-historical artefacts that are simultaneously products of human psychology and productive of cognitive effects. As I've discussed at length in other publications, the existential problem of 'separation' (explicitly linked to the psychology of attachment, abandonment and loss) is a focus of considerable attention across Chinese ritual, literature, art, popular culture, daily life and other domains. Indeed, it can be argued that this existential problem is elaborated in all human cultures, an historical outcome driven by our psychological tendency as humans to intuitively care about attachment (just as Bowlby predicted). In the particular case of China, cultural-historical artefacts that deal in some way with the problem of human separation – and its corollary, reunion – are highly pervasive, to be sure (see Stafford 2000, 2003). Mrs Lin knows this well, because it directly informs her daily practice as a spirit medium. In short, a large proportion of Chinese ritual acts *are* acts of separation and reunion (e.g. the 'sending off' and 'greeting' of ancestors and other spirits during the New Year celebrations), not to mention that a high proportion of everyday medium activities at Mrs Lin's altar address either the threat or the reality of abandonment and loss.

Meanwhile, drowning has traditionally been seen in China as an especially bad type of death, specifically because the body may never be recovered and buried, which makes it impossible for proper rituals of 'reunion' and family inclusion to be held (thus it is that the issues of separation and drowning converge). In line with this, the coastline around Angang is considered highly dangerous at certain spots because the spirits of angry drowning victims lurk there, ready to grab passers-by. Every local child will know ghost stories of this kind. Moreover, one of Mrs Lin's own relatives had died from drowning while on a fishing trip in the not-too-distant past. The presence of his widow in their daily lives – she was a devotee at Mr Su's altar – reminded everyone of what was at stake every time boats went to sea. To lose one's husband to drowning would be a terrible fate (by which I mean that loss in general is bad, but loss via drowning is considered especially bad). Further to this, the generally risk-averse orientation of the Chinese family system manifests itself in a wide range of cultural practices (including those centred on spirit-medium altars) designed precisely to avert a calamity of this kind – something that, by the way, arguably increases rather than decreases the anxiety people feel about it possibly happening (Stafford 2007).

In sum, as these brief comments suggest, the emotions impinging on decision making are simultaneously psychological and cultural-historical phenomena. That is, they are individually felt but also inextricably caught up with a wide range of 'mind-external' artefacts such as rituals – so much so that the internal-external dichotomy surely collapses.

But exactly what role do our culturally shaped and elaborated emotions play in economic life? Here let me turn briefly to a different kind of psychological evidence. We often speak as if emotions interfere with effective decision making, of course. However, the neuropsychologist Antonio Damasio has argued that our ability to reason and take decisions evolved, in fact, from the automatic emotional system through which our ancestors responded to challenges in their environment (Damasio 2006 [1994]; for an accessible overview of some work in this field, see also Öhman 2006). His basic conclusion is that when we as (modern) humans make decisions, this emotional system *needs* to be engaged.[12] The evidence for this comes from patients who have 'lost affect' due to brain injuries, i.e. whose emotional systems are impaired. Some of them retain very good levels of general intelligence, but what they cannot do is experience emotions in the normal way. One consequence of this is that they are often bad, sometimes catastrophically so, at making decisions, especially in what Damasio refers to as the 'personal/social' domain.[13] Basically, they cannot feel (and thus intuitively judge) what the personal/social consequences of a particular course of action might be.

In relation to my own concerns here, two points about Damasio's argument might be noted. The first is that what he calls the 'personal/social' domain is closely linked, in neuropsychological terms, both to emotional processing *and* to decision making. The second point is that with respect to all three of these phenomena – that is, when it comes to (1) us being social, (2) us having feelings/emotions and (3) us taking decisions – we rely heavily on the learned (i.e. culturally transmitted) rules, norms and expectations that govern collective experience. Here again, notionally

---

[12] To put it simply, Damasio argues that feelings and emotions help guide decision making by 'marking' (at a conscious or unconscious level) certain features of a situation as relevant and worthy of attention. This is known as the 'somatic marker hypothesis' (2006: 165–201). More specifically, Damasio hypothesises (among other things) that 'the somatic-state mechanism acts as a booster to maintain and optimize working memory and attention concerned with scenarios of the future' (2006: 219). For an overview and a critical evaluation of this hypothesis, see Dunn et al. (2006).

[13] As Damasio puts it, 'When emotion is entirely left out of the reasoning picture, as happens in certain neurological conditions, reason turns out to be even more flawed than [it is] when emotions play bad tricks in our decisions' (2006: xviii). In reality, whether an impairment of the emotions is 'good' or 'bad' for decision making depends on the kinds of decisions being taken, and under what conditions. But under the normal conditions of human social life, Damasio suggests, such impairment has devastating effects. For a more general discussion of risk and decision making that draws on Damasio's theories, see Slovic et al. (2004).

mind-internal and mind-external phenomena are linked. In describing a famous case from the neuropsychology literature, Damasio observes that the patient – who after a brain injury lost the ability to experience emotions normally – seems thereby to have lost as well the ability to 'conduct himself according to the social rules he previously had learned' (2006: 33). As a result, the patient 'lost something uniquely human, the ability to plan his future as a social being' (2006:19).

* * *

Taking a lead from Damasio, then, the problem can be framed bio-graphically. The life stories of people in Angang are caught up in rela-tions with others – including parents, spouses, children, friends, etc. In simple terms, religious practice is about asking the gods to provide *ping an* – meaning 'peace' or, more literally, 'the absence of problems' – for oneself and the people with whom one is caught up in webs of inter-action and mutual dependency. Partly as a result of this, religious life is intensely emotional. It entails dramatic, even dangerous, practices: spirit mediums cutting themselves with knives and swords during pos-session episodes, fire-walking rituals that ordinary devotees are compelled to participate in, boisterous public processions that take over the whole community (including private households and businesses) and so on. The motive to engage in such practices comes from emotions generated within the realm of family life and, to a lesser extent, close friendship – i.e. from the deeply felt desire to protect the people one loves and therefore to pro-tect one's own life story from the spectre of failure and abandonment. The same is true of day-to-day activities at private spirit-medium altars: devotees go there to deal with a range of problems, virtually all of which come from within, or relate directly to, the family or other intimate relationships. They sincerely hope that the techniques of divination and intervention supplied by mediums will work. Indeed, it might be said that while the 'problem of trusting others' (including the problem of worrying about the intentions of mediums) is pushing them in one direction – towards disbelief – the emotional force of private life, and of culturally constituted aspirations for it and fears about it, is pushing them in the opposite direction, i.e. towards entrusting their lives, their futures as social beings, to the gods and following their advice in deciding what to do. And perhaps the artefact I mentioned earlier gives them another push in this direction.

As I noted near the start of the chapter, however, the fishing-trip decisions made by Mr Lin and Mr Su in this case – whatever role divination may have played in them – are consistent with a relatively simple logic of risk and reward, taking their family circumstances into account. And Taiwan is a market-oriented society. In their everyday activities and conversations, people in Angang show that they are more than aware of this and all that it implies, e.g. they speak knowledgeably about supply, demand, price, competition, risk and so on. They articulate a clear folk model of what it is logical for different kinds of family units, based in a capitalist society, to do in order to advance their economic interests. One could thus argue that religion, whatever it may achieve, does little to interfere with the underlying psychology of local economic agents.

Here it may help to distinguish, however, between different categories of individuals. There are a certain number of people in Angang who are 'literalists': devout believers who are inclined to simply take advice from the gods – whatever it may be – and apply it to life directly, even if it blatantly contradicts their self-interest. There are also some people who don't believe in the gods at all and who consider spirit mediumship and other forms of divination to be a complete fraud (whether such people are rational in economic life is another question, obviously). This leaves those, probably the majority, who are neither literalists nor full-blown sceptics. What happens to them? One possibility (to return to Astuti's discussion of situational beliefs) is that they take economic decisions primarily in an 'economics frame of mind', e.g. because the context leads them to focus their thoughts on potential risks and financial rewards. And then what they think/believe when communicating with gods about economic matters is something else altogether. Of course, the problem comes if and when they have to reconcile contradictory outcomes obtained in these two contexts. For example, a fisherman might decide (in 'economics mode') to go on a trip because of the money to be made, but then divination procedures (carried out while in 'religious mode') might tell him that it is too dangerous. He could discount one of the outcomes based on his weighting of them, but here the possibility of manipulation (discussed previously) also comes into play. That is, the fisherman might actively *try* to obtain an answer from the gods that is consistent with what he thinks would be for the best – i.e. as judged in 'economics mode'. Plus, the medium he consults may feel implicit or explicit pressure to provide him with the answers she thinks that he, the paying customer, is looking for …

Putting matters in this way, however, has the effect of making religion sound like a peripheral consideration when it comes to 'real' economic life and 'real' economic decision making: that is, because it can always, in the end, be manipulated so as not to contradict economic logic. In the case of Angang, at least, I would argue strongly against this conclusion. For one thing, there are quite a few literalists there, devout believers who simply take their instructions from the gods. And among the bulk of non-literalist believers, there are many who would weight divination outcomes, whatever these may be, quite heavily when deciding what to do. Indeed, even practicing sceptics in Angang may leave decisions to the gods in some circumstances, not least because this is one way (however arbitrary) of resolving an unresolved question, of bringing closure.

* * *

Meanwhile, a crucial factor in all of this, to go back to the earlier discussion, is the fundamentally social nature of decision making. Divination (whether undertaken by literalists, sceptics or those in-between) is part of a wider public conversation not only about what one ought to do in life, but also about the moral and ethical implications of it. To return to

Mercier and Sperber's formulation, the kind of thing I've been describing could be understood as (public) reasoning about economic activity for social and 'argumentative' purposes, as much as for the sake of arriving at decisions. Consider, for example, some (non-mutually exclusive) reasons a fisherman in Angang might give for *not* making a proposed trip to the Philippines:

1. Because the weather forecast looks bad.
2. Because my family situation is such that I don't need to go on risky long-distance fishing trips anymore.
3. Because my wife told me not to go.
4. Because the god advised against it.

Note that although 1 and 2 seem relatively straightforward and logical, both are subject to debate and interpretation. Indeed, because such things are debated and discussed very often in public contexts, this is one way in which information (e.g. about the reliability of weather forecasts) is circulated in the community. Moreover, reason 2, in particular, is clearly dependent on culturally specific ways of seeing the world – including those related to family goals and aspirations. To debate and discuss it is therefore, in part, a way of agreeing what our view of the world actually is. Reason 3, meanwhile, is one that is widely given in Angang; but it is potentially problematic. On the one hand, local men are well aware that Angang women have a reputation for toughness, and sometimes even joke and/or brag about this. On the other hand, they know that within the Chinese tradition men should be household heads, and submission to one's wife in decision making could thus be seen as a humiliation. In some cases, it might be strategic to invoke one's wife as an excuse for doing or not doing a particular thing (because in most circumstances listeners in Angang will simply accept this as a valid reason); but there can also be a price to pay for it, e.g. in terms of one's standing among male peers. And then, as should already be clear from my discussion, reason 4 is complicated as well. Note, however, that *when* people give divine justifications for action in Angang, these are particularly difficult ones to argue against. Of course, different individuals might have varied reactions on hearing such a justification, including 'I don't believe in the gods, so this is a ridiculous reason not to go' or 'I don't trust the particular medium who transmitted this advice, so I don't accept that it should be followed'. But to say such things publicly and forcefully in Angang, at least in many contexts at the time of my fieldwork, would be to make a serious challenge – against a given medium and/or against the relatives, friends and neighbours who are the clients of this medium and/or even against the norms of local society as a whole.

* * *

And thus it is that some cultural-historical artefacts related to religious life – including the notions that 'important decisions should be put to the gods' and that 'spirit mediums should not act, when possessed, in their own self-interest' – have some role in the economy of Angang. Putting decisions before the gods implies that we *believe* in them, but religious belief is a complex psychological phenomenon (as the accounts of Mercier and Sperber, Astuti, Bloch and others show). So too is the activity of trusting and doubting the people around us who specialise in religious activity, including spirit mediums – something that is shaped, in part, by the *emotions* we feel as part of living in the social and cultural worlds in which we are situated and which provide us with our basic moral and ethical bearings.

But here let me return to what I said in the Introduction: that the process whereby we end up with the psychological attributes that impinge on our economic agency – including our beliefs and emotions – is intrinsically historical. As I've indicated, most people in Angang come to believe in the gods propelled in that direction not just by general cultural learning but also by the emotional force of private life. This is a matter of personal biography; e.g. in the case of Mrs Su it relates specifically to the fact that her (beloved) father was a medium. But during her lifetime, there have also been many changes to Taiwanese religious practice and the context in which it occurs, not least as a result of government campaigns (direct and indirect) against 'superstition'. And the artefacts outlined here that militate against scepticism – themselves historical products – are of course never detached from the individual and collective histories unfolding around them.

But allow me to give a somewhat more extended example, this one related to kinship rather than religion. As I've explained, Mr Su's son (employed locally) lives with his parents rather than having left them behind, as many young people from Angang have done. One way or another, he ended up feeling responsible for what happened to them – an emotional phenomenon. Not only this, he was able to convince his Taipei-born wife that she should give up a life in the city in order to care for *his* ageing parents in the small, relatively remote fishing community of Angang. And his wife had to be able to convince *her* parents that these arrangements were acceptable, and they had to let her go. Interestingly, the parents in Taipei must have played a part, as well, in giving her the disposition not to mind too much being stuck for a while in the classic role of the 'married-in' Chinese daughter-in-law – which requires a good deal of subservience. I found this odd, because in other respects she seemed very modern. But during my fieldwork, this bright and often-assertive young woman was a kind of servant (as she cheerfully told me) in the house of her parents-in-law, so it is just as well that she liked them very much. She had, for example, to sit and watch quietly while her mother-in-law disciplined her own daughter in ways that she may not personally have found very nice – thereby increasing, by a small increment, this mother-in-law's (i.e. Mrs Su's) sense that life was on track, i.e. that the future was unfolding as she would want. So why take risks? What need for her husband to make a dangerous fishing trip to the Philippines?

My point is that to arrive at this conclusion, and thus for it to factor in decision making, requires a complicated chain of learning and emotional transactions to have taken place, e.g. on the part of Mr Su's son and his wife and also between them. But the point is also that such processes of learning are, again, always historically situated. That this is true may be seen in one detail in the story: the fact that the Sus' grandchild is a *girl*. Traditionally, of course, what was wanted in China and Taiwan was for one's sons to have sons. Nothing short of this would have had a very big impact on the kind of economic decision I'm discussing. As is well known, however, attitudes have changed in recent decades, so that now many people accept – at the end of a complex learning curve – that having daughters may be more financially and emotionally rewarding than in the past, and in some respects even better than having sons.

But there's something specific, and slightly paradoxical, to the learning of this in Angang. Angang is a place in which there have traditionally been a relatively large number of 'local' and formally uxorilocal marriages, i.e. ones in which daughters stay close to, or actually live with, their natal families after marriage. They therefore interact with and rely upon their natal families throughout life, and also contribute quite a bit more back to these families than the traditional Chinese model (based on virilocal residence) might have predicted. In a community of this kind, then, people long ago learned that the traditional stereotype of sons and grandsons being more important than daughters and granddaughters is not necessarily borne out in practice. Indeed, as I've said, Mr Su's own sister, Mrs Lin, lives a short distance from his home, and they interact regularly. It might therefore be hard for him to picture his granddaughter as 'water poured on the ground' (a traditional expression meant to convey the total loss to a family of girls once they marry).

Interestingly, however, residence patterns have been changing and, as noted, both of Mr Su's daughters have moved elsewhere in Taiwan rather than settling locally. This is partly for career reasons but also because 'local' marriages have increasingly been seen as low prestige in Angang (as in Taiwan and China more generally). So, paradoxically, while the modern trend across Taiwan is clearly towards greater valuation of daughters, modernity in Angang means going towards a form of marriage which is somewhat *more* traditional (in the sense of moving brides away from their natal homes) and therefore arguably *less* amenable to high daughter valuation. This kind of detail is important, because it reminds us that kinship is a field of contestation – not just tradition – and one in which individual choices and actions have the potential to be transformative in the course of history.

In any case, it happens that in Angang women's power is visible in daily life (notwithstanding the 'servant' status of married-in daughters-in-law), and this is something everybody can see and learn from, including Mr Su's granddaughter. For example, she sat by my side watching her grandmother (a woman) mock her grandfather (a man) for suggesting that he could take a decision about fishing in the Philippines without her consent. And she has undoubtedly observed situations like the one I described a moment ago, in which her aunt, Mrs Lin, was mocked by her own young daughter for crying when her husband was at sea. Angang women are meant to be independent and tough, after all, not weepy – as the local women teach each other. Such things do, in the end, have economic implications, in part by providing the emotional and ethical backdrop to the 'logical' consideration of alternatives.

I also might add that she (again, the granddaughter) sat by my side one afternoon as her grandfather told me how he had come to be a fisherman – and thus to know whatever it is that fishermen know. He said it was partly because, as a boy, he enjoyed skipping school and had gone fishing instead. But it was also because his own father could not afford to keep him in school in spite of the fact that his examination results had actually been rather good. He thus became a fisherman, which – he claimed with a grin – is basically the most 'pathetic' job in the world. Be that as it may, what his granddaughter learns and knows today is tied not only to these elements of his own personal history, but also – as with the two children from Protected Mountain with whom I started the Introduction – to the wider *collective* history that produced modern Angang and that frames the possibilities of learning and decision making for people there now.

∗ ∗ ∗

Given all this historical particularity, readers may wonder about the comment I made at the start of the chapter. I indicated that my point here is ultimately a universalist one, and that the material I am presenting is not so much about people in Taiwan – who happen to be religious in their uniquely Taiwanese way – but rather about you. What did I have in mind? I presume that all of us would accept that humans everywhere live in culture and history, and that cultural learning (shaped by the artefacts in our cognitive environments) matters a lot for who we turn out to be. This is true for people who are living in Taiwanese fishing villages, to be sure, but equally true for the people who are living around me in London as I write this book – including those who work in the City of London as professional economists, to give but one example. In brief, when it comes to the human species, culture always matters. I don't think this should be controversial.

Beyond this, however, I would add two more specific points:

• The economic psychology of all of us, everywhere, is shaped by cultural-historical artefacts that relate specifically to family and kinship – in some cases, in spite of us living apart from our closest relatives for years or even decades at a time. And although the family and kinship artefacts I have referred to in this chapter are, of course, particular to a given culture and society at a given moment, everybody everywhere will live with some version of these artefacts.

One difficulty with fully appreciating the importance of this first point, however, is that in the contemporary West there is a powerful ideology that suggests that our societies are *not* organised around kinship anymore, and that family life has essentially become a private domain of restricted public consequence. In a range of important senses, this is totally misleading (McKinnon & Cannell 2013). It's not as if 'they', the people out there in places such as Taiwan, have families and we don't, but rather that the kinship we live with is not always the same as theirs – and of course sometimes it is radically different. By extension, just as their cultural-historical artefacts of kinship have demonstrable consequences for their economic psychology, helping determine what they do in the world, our artefacts of kinship have demonstrable consequences for our economic psychology, helping determine what we do in the world.

• And then, more controversially, I want to argue that everybody everywhere is 'religious', and that this is universally relevant for economic psychology and economic agency as well.

Most academics live in majority non-religious bubbles and predominantly think of themselves as non-religious, which means that this second point is hard to convey – I would say actually harder than the (quite hard-to-convey) first point about kinship. Outside of such bubbles, however, the human world is definitively religious on the whole. Measuring religious belief and practice is notoriously hard, but a recent Pew Research Center report suggests that fully 84 per cent of people in the world claim a religious affiliation of some kind (Pew Research Center 2012). It might be felt that 'affiliation' is such a weak word as to be meaningless, but what is striking about this finding is that the people *without* such a self-ascribed affiliation are so clearly in the minority (i.e. just 16 per cent). Moreover, even those who do not affiliate with a religion at all are still certain to be heavily influenced in their thinking – including in relation to their 'logical' deliberation about life choices – by religious/moral values that permeate the societies in which they live. Post-Mao China is an interesting case in this regard. The figures for religious affiliation per se are relatively low, as one would predict in light of official attacks on religious belief and practice that took place there over a period of many decades. But this very much depends on how 'religion' is defined, and it turns out that a significant proportion of people in China *do* participate in activities, such as hiring geomancers or offering incense to ancestral spirits, that fall within the folk-religion category, while not affiliating per se with any religion. Moreover, it can be argued that even in the total absence of religious practice of any kind, we still find that the values coming from religion have permeated Chinese society. Further to this, I believe that – at least for the purpose of this discussion – we should include not only those who are actively religious but also those who hold a transcendent moral and ethical sense of the kind that everywhere underpins the creation of the social. As I have already explained, this is what religion is about in the Durkheimian view (note also that there are more recent evolutionary explanations for the resilience of religious thinking across human societies, cf. Johnson 2016). And if we do allow this broader Durkheimian (and/or evolutionary) account of what 'religion' is actually doing in human societies, we would end up with a universal or near universal.

In sum, then, although this chapter could be read as a classic anthropological exercise in drawing attention to other ways of living, this has not been my goal. My goal has been to remind us of some basic facts about humans in general: that cultural-historical artefacts always matter for us, and universally so (I am claiming) in the domains of kinship and religion.

But does any of this matter for economists and/or economic psychologists? Some economists have studied religion, to be sure, and actually *many* economists have studied family life and kinship in one form or another – a very famous illustration of the latter being Gary Becker's contributions to the field of 'family economics' (Becker 1993b; for a summary and critical overview, see Pollak 2002). In short, it's not as if these topics have been ignored by economists – on the contrary. So far as economists such as Becker are concerned, however, the whole point is that they can take their *economics approach* – which centrally entails *not* having to take 'everything' into account, in the manner of anthropologists – and then apply this to the study of literally anything. Becker himself labelled this 'the economic way of looking at life' (Becker 1993a), and others have referred to it (sometimes with pride) as economics imperialism (Lazear 2000). In brief, the key assumption behind this is that human activity in any domain can be explained with reference to some version of rational-choice theory. That is, whatever type of activity people out there in the real world are engaged in, they will be seeking to maximise their utility or welfare 'as they conceive it'. The last bit of this sentence – a phrase from Becker – is crucial from an anthropological point of view. In short, economists claim that they *don't* need to know where an agent's conception of utility or welfare has come from: it could be from their immersion in religion or in family life, to be sure, but there are an endless number of possible sources of it. To an anthropologist, this sounds like a very strange way of proceeding, i.e. because it involves ignoring what makes people what they are. But the economics approach is at least logically coherent, as I will explain in Chapter 3, and it does massively simplify social analysis.

Still, it's interesting to reflect on the very different impacts that the 'psychological' and the 'cultural' critiques of standard economics have had. The interdisciplinary economic psychology critique of economics has had a big impact, as I've explained. Not every economist accepts it, by any means, but it has changed the way in which many of them – perhaps most of them – think about the representative economic agent on which their work is premised. All humans have an evolved psychology that leads them to think and act in ways that are *not* in line with the assumptions of most economic models – and this is potentially relevant to *anything* that an economist might want to study. All I am adding here is the old anthropological truism that the thinking and deciding of humans is (always) heavily influenced by the cultural-historical artefacts to be found in their cognitive environments, and universally so in the domains of kinship and religion. However, this comes with a

major complication, which is that the artefacts themselves are culturally and historically variable. In other words, humans have one evolved
psychology but many cultures. One could build (or at least try to build)
the existence of cognitive biases and dispositions into economic models,
and these could then – at least in principle – be applied universally. But
such a thing cannot be done with respect to the artefacts of kinship and
religion. This helps explain, I think, why mainstream economists have
been very influenced by the behavioural revolution but hardly touched
at all by the ideas about 'embeddedness' that have come from anthropology and related disciplines. The message from the anthropologists –
however true – just doesn't help economists do what they are trying to
do. Even if they were to agree that, in theory, cultural-historical artefacts
of kinship and religion should be as important for economic agents as
the biases and dispositions that psychologists have studied, they would
have no efficient way of dealing with this information. The problem is
that ignoring this information is also not entirely satisfactory. It means
leaving out some of what is most important about being a human and
experiencing life as an economic agent in the real world, such as the fact
of us being a 'religious' species. In any case, I do understand and accept
why economists proceed in the way that they do. Meanwhile, however,
it is less clear to me why the behavioural psychology revolution in economics has not been matched by a cultural-historical revolution in
economic psychology.

THREE

Substantivist Economic Psychology

As explained in Chapter 2, popular religion plays an obvious role when it comes to economic decision making in Angang. Certainly, ordinary people there *talk* as if the most important decisions in their lives, and quite a few of the minor ones as well, are taken by gods rather than by rational human agents. Indeed, in many human communities around the world – including those in the rural US 'heartland' where I have recently been doing fieldwork – the same kind of thing is said. In other words, the phenomenon I am drawing attention to, i.e. of religion having consequences for economic life, is not a marginal or exotic one by any means. As I have also indicated, the phenomenon of *kinship* being consequential for economic life is not restricted to the so-called traditional societies. On the contrary, this is just how we, as humans, live.

But let us assume, for a moment, that economists do not want to get bogged down in such things, i.e. that they do not want to turn themselves into fieldworking anthropologists in order to study religious beliefs and/or kinship practices in all their rich variety. As noted, I presume that economists would take the (intentionally rambling) case study in Chapter 2 as illustrating nicely why they *avoid* bringing real-world ethnographic data into their analyses. After all, where our values and preferences come from, and what they are, is not the main concern of economists. More specifically, most economists just take such things as being exogenously given (cf. Dietrich & List 2012). This approach, with its simplifying assumptions, can moreover be used to study *anything*, including kinship and religion. Whereas if we decide that *everything* – including culturally variable religious beliefs and kinship practices of the kind that anthropologists study via immersive fieldwork – needs to be incorporated into the economics approach itself, there is basically never going to be an end to it. You might end up having to incorporate the arcane rules of Taiwanese divination and who knows what else. Of course, the same thing can be said about incorporating human psychology into economic analyses: once you start, there is never going to be end to that either.

These two things being so, economists need some strategies for coping with the cultural *and* psychological complexities that, as they understand perfectly well, do exist in the world. Actually, when it comes to cultural-historical variation, one very simple strategy is to restrict oneself to speaking only of modern Western capitalism – thus avoiding, for example, the question of what "utility maximising" might look like for people in other times and in very different kinds of places (e.g. for Melanesians who were caught up in the cycles of the traditional gift economy). A different strategy is to adopt a kind of soft universalism. While not denying that economic life may vary in space and time (e.g. that the traditional Melanesian gift economy is not the same kind of thing as consumer capitalism in Europe), one can still argue that it shares some basic common features, e.g. that labour inputs have to be reproduced, somehow, that certain agricultural goods will always be more perishable than others and so on. Of course, anthropologists frown on universalism of any kind. And yet there are defensible reasons for adopting at least a soft version of it in relation to the analysis of economic life.

But it is really the psychological questions that have vexed economists in recent years, much more so than the questions about cultural-historical variation. To paraphrase Solow, real-world human psychology is vastly too complicated for economists to ever properly grasp. The question is how best to cope with this – and preferably without having to turn oneself into a full-fledged psychologist. The *rationalist* response, as I have explained in the Introduction, entails making some 'unrealistic' assumptions as a starting point for modelling. One can assume that economic agents are perfectly rational (even if they aren't), that their preferences never change (even if they do), that they have perfect information about the market (even if they don't) and so on. And just to be very clear, these are not mistakes but rather modelling assumptions. A somewhat less radical approach – in the sense that it is more realistic – is to adopt a version of *behaviourism*. This means focusing on the observable and measurable actions of real-world agents (such as them actually making a purchase) rather than on the complex, even baffling mental processes that might have led up to these. Who knows what these people are thinking! Fortunately, we don't need to know. A third response is to always take human psychology and human behaviour on *aggregate*, i.e. at the level of groups (preferably very big ones), thus ironing out the idiosyncrasies of individual preferences, motives, decisions, actions and so on. Whether working at the micro level of individual firms or at the macro level of national economies, economists can be said to do all of these things to some extent. That is, they are rationalists to some extent (content to adopt 'unrealistic' assumptions in the service of model-building, and indeed viewing this as a necessary first step); they are behaviourists to some extent (more concerned with what people do than with the messy detail of what they think or feel before acting); and they are statistical aggregators to some extent (more concerned with broad/aggregate patterns than with statistically trivial variations and individual idiosyncrasies).

* * *

Of course, an anthropologist would probably feel that in adopting strategies of these kinds – which undoubtedly simplify the process of model-building – economists manage to miss much of what is most interesting, indeed crucial, about economic life as it is actually experienced by real human beings. But then it has to be admitted that anthropologists, too, have their own strategies for dealing with complications they would prefer not to get bogged down in. In particular – and not unlike the economists – they routinely bracket off human psychology, leaving open the question of how human learning, beliefs, emotions, decisions, etc., contribute to the behavioural patterns we observe in the course of fieldwork.

With respect to this, it may be useful to briefly discuss the legacy of Max Weber. As every anthropologist knows, Weber profoundly influenced the 'culturalist' strand of economic anthropology. It is probably much less well known, at least by anthropologists, that Weber had serious interests in theoretical economics – and actually self-identified as an economist throughout his career (see Swedberg 1999). As for the cultural side of Weber's work, he was famously interested in the question of how the actions of individuals are motivated by the culturally specific values and beliefs they have come to hold. In *The Protestant Ethic*, he argued that Calvinists were led by their (culturally constituted) anxieties about predestination and salvation to behave in particular ways: to save and invest money rather than spending it, e.g. on consumption. This, in turn, may have contributed to the emergence of capitalism in northern Europe.

On the surface, at least, Weber's telling of this story about early capitalism places individual psychology at the heart of historical-sociological analysis. That is, he draws an explicit link between (a) cultural-historical determinants (such as religious beliefs), (b) the private emotions of individuals (in this case, anxiety about predestination) and (c) the history-making actions of these people (such as saving money). But Weber, like Durkheim, explicitly rejects the idea that a better understanding of *psychology* per se will help human scientists account for what takes place in the social worlds we study. According to commentators, his anti-psychologism was a reaction to some of the specific theories, findings and methods that were circulating in his own time and that he was strongly dismissive of, including the 'psychophysics' of Fechner and Wundt. But the deeper objection is more generalisable, it seems. Briefly, Weber holds that while psychology may be useful with respect to explaining the 'internal sensations' of individuals, what it *cannot* explain are the 'external actions' through which social actors respond to the circumstances in which they find themselves (see Levine 2005).

But exactly how *should* one understand the causes of our external actions? According to Weber, these can be understood – at least for ideal-typical purposes – as the outcome of evaluations individuals make of the available 'means' they have in relation to desired 'ends'. In other words, we decide what to do by figuring out the best way of getting what it is we want. More specifically, as the economic historian Harro Maas explains, Weber holds that *any* rational individual will be able to rank such means objectively and then act accordingly so as to achieve his ends. In effect, both the means and the ends are 'mind external', i.e. out there in the environment, while the 'mind-internal' process of reasoning about them is explained via the assumption of rationality. It follows from this that knowing more about the (presumably highly variable) internal mental states of individuals will not help us at all in our sociological analyses. As Maas puts it, once rationality is assumed 'no assessment [needs] to be made [i.e. for Weber's purposes] of the psychology of the individual' (Maas 2009: 508). Weber himself puts things a bit more bluntly. When it was suggested that marginal utility theory (which, in Weber's view, *could* provide a framework for explaining human action) ought to be reduced to a branch of experimental psychology, he replied that this theory 'has in my opinion nothing more to do with "psychology" than with astronomy or I don't know what else' (Weber cited in Levine 2005: 105; see also Weber 1975a, 1975b, 1981).[1]

---

[1] As Louis Schneider explains in his translator's introduction to Weber's essay about marginal utility, 'Weber is concerned to demonstrate that economic theory, with special reference to marginal utility analysis, is in no way dependent on psychological theorems, principles or concepts. Weber simply sees economic theory as an enterprise working out the consequences of assumptions of economic rationality on the part of economic agents, precisely in purely analytical terms and again independently of any psychology whatsoever' (1975a: 22). It is interesting to compare the (similar) stance of Weber's contemporary Pareto (see Bruni & Sugden 2007). Note that the economist Lionel Robbins, among others, drew on Weber in developing his own (rather different) account of why economics, in particular, should remain detached from psychology (Maas 2009).

The key point to note is that although anthropologists think of Weber as an anti-universalist par excellence – thanks in particular to the influence of *The Protestant Ethic* – he in fact subscribed to a version of rational-choice theory, which he saw as a tractable and widely applicable model of human agency. However, a couple of crucial riders to this should be borne in mind. The first is that Weber does *not* believe (and nor, so far as I know, does any economist) that humans are always rational. His model of rational action is, again, explicitly ideal typical and aggregative. The second is that Weber *does* believe (and probably much more strongly than the average economist) that the kind of rationality we find under modern capitalism is at least in part historically specific. As Zafirovski puts it, Weber's underlying or 'latent' point in his writings on the subject is that utility-maximising *homo economicus* is an artefact of 'the historical peculiarity of modern capitalism' rather than being a universal phenomenon (Zafirovski 2001: 442). But these two crucial riders still, I would suggest, leave anthropologists in an uncomfortable position with regard to Weber's legacy. It goes without saying that they admire his stress on the cultural-historical specificity of economic life and of modern capitalism in particular. They presumably also admire and accept Weber's argument that the human sciences should not be reduced to the study of individual psychology. However, the Weber of means/ends rationality is another thing. His commitment to (in effect) a rational-choice model of human action, even if restricted to modern capitalism, is strongly at odds with most anthropological understandings: it makes him sound like an economist! Moreover, the behavioural economics revolution that in recent years has undermined the rationality assumptions of standard economics has surely *also* undermined the rationality assumptions of Max Weber.

* * *

But this brings me to a question. Would it be better to have an ideal-typical model of rationality, decision making and action of the kind formulated by Weber and others and applied (in different permutations) by economists over the decades – even if this is discredited by subsequent empirical research – or to have no working model at all? The position in anthropology is arguably the latter. That is, we tend to jump straight from the cultural-historical artefacts found in the cognitive environments where humans live to activity that is presumed to be motivated by these artefacts – but without pausing to specify at all the (psychological) mechanism whereby the former actually leads to the latter.

How should this gap be addressed? One option for anthropologists is to deny that psychology plays any crucial role in human affairs, or at least to say it is irrelevant at the social/cultural level that we focus on in our research work – which means that it can be left out of our accounts (the latter was basically Geertz's position). However, given the turn of anthropology in recent decades towards a sustained focus on phenomena such as learning, memory, emotion, subjectivity, identity, moral judgement and so on, this option has surely become much harder to sustain. If we truly wanted to ignore psychology, perhaps we should have stuck with the study of 'culture' and/or 'social structure' as pure abstractions. Of course, it might still be claimed that what human agents think, know, believe, etc., is *determined* by the cultural-historical environments in which they live – thus rendering individual psychology moot. But our own ethnographic evidence consistently shows strong cultural determinism of this kind to be completely untenable. Surely no anthropologist believes that Confucianism, to give one example, determines in any simple sense what individuals in China and Taiwan think or do in relation to economic life, even if it is true that it influences what some people think and do, some of the time.

A middle ground would be to adopt some version of the methodological individualism inspired – precisely – by Weber, e.g. along the lines proposed by Barth (in anthropology) and Granovetter (in sociology), without venturing into full-blown rational-choice theory.[2] This position

---

[2] Heath (2015) provides a very useful and succinct overview of methodological individualism, including the political debates surrounding it.

also rejects psychologism. But at least it acknowledges, along with Weber, that when we talk about a culture or society or community of people 'valuing something' or 'doing something', we are referring to the aggregate values and actions of *thinking individuals*. Note that a strong version of methodological individualism would lead us to focus on the intentions and actions of these thinking individuals: to really go psychological. But as Granovetter (1985) points out, there is a risk that an approach of this kind will be 'under-socialised', i.e. not enough weight will be given to social constraints and cultural constructions, whereas too much weight will be given to individual psychology and action alone. Meanwhile, a weak version of methodological individualism presents the opposite risk: that we will come up with an 'over-socialised' picture in which everything anyone thinks or does is simply determined by social and cultural factors. In short, the first approach risks ignoring society, culture and history, and the second approach risks ignoring psychology and individual agency.

Both Granovetter and Barth try to square this circle by focusing on aggregate patterns of observable behaviour, which can be taken as a kind of behaviourist proxy for what the people think, on average. As Barth (1967) notes, most anthropologists do, in any case, engage in implicit statistical aggregation of this kind, e.g. when they write about a culture having this or that value or of a people as having collectively 'done' something. What can be helpful is to make this explicit, which is the approach advocated by the economic anthropologist Michael Chibnik, whose work on economic choice I have discussed in Chapter 2. As noted, Chibnik came to reject the rational-choice framework, having tried to apply it to his early fieldwork material. But he is also dubious about the 'culturalist' (i.e. cultural determinist) accounts of economic life put forward by many anthropologists (2011: 8–9; cf. the review of Chibnik's book by Wilk 2013). Moreover, Chibnik – as a mainstream sociocultural anthropologist of economy – is dubious about the attempts that realist psychological/evolutionary anthropologists (specifically, Joseph Henrich and Naomi Quinn) have made to generate better accounts of economic decision making as a psychological phenomenon. What he argues for, instead, is a statistical/aggregative approach, i.e. one based on observed behavioural outcomes that can be quantified – the point being that we can, in this way, avoid the black box of what people think before they act and instead simply focus (as do non-behavioural economists, in their empirical work) on what they do (Chibnik 1980, 2011).

I personally have more sympathy for methodological individualism as an approach than do most contemporary anthropologists, and I also find Chibnik's statistical-behavioural approach very interesting and worthwhile. To be more specific, what I admire is Chibnik's *coherent* attempt to tackle 'the individual psychology problem' by means of behaviourism rather than simply evading it. And yet his is still ultimately a non-psychological approach, which means that a good deal is missing from it. It simplifies anthropological analysis by bracketing off individual psychology, which does have advantages, to be sure. Along the way, however, we lose sight of the core psychological mechanisms on which economic agency as we know it rests. Given that anthropologists are happy to treat 'everything' as potentially bearing on economic life, why leave the particulars of human psychology out of the picture? It seems arbitrary, to say the least.

* * *

In my view, the solution to the psychology problem in anthropology is actually relatively simple. (Having said this, I should note that there are ideological barriers to anthropologists giving ground on this subject, as I will discuss in Chapter 6.) First, as per my discussion in Chapter 2, we should stop thinking of culture as something that only *acts on psychology*, as opposed to it being something that is *acted upon by psychology*. Anthropologists have long argued that our shared cultures influence (even to some extent determine) the psychology of humans: what we think, what we know, even what we feel. This is a profound fact about the human species, i.e. that we are constantly caught up in cultural learning and that this ultimately makes us what we are – in a deep sense. But as Lévi-Strauss taught us, the cultural-historical artefacts we find in human societies are *themselves* acted on and constrained by how we as humans think, i.e. by our psychology and by the particulars of learning and cultural transmission in our species. Without psychology, the relevant artefacts could not ever have come into existence, they could not be reproduced, they could not be transformed and nor could they continue to be relevant to our everyday lives. In short, just as culture shapes human thought, so too does human thought profoundly shape the cultures we end up living with.

Second, we should stop thinking of human psychology as intrinsically 'individual', i.e. as something going on inside of people's heads. With respect to this, it's worth noting that economics and psychology as human science disciplines are considerably less interested in *individual* psychology and *individual* rationality than many anthropologists tend to assume. As a matter of routine, anthropologists accuse economists of being obsessed with 'individual rational choosers', but it is surely anthropologists who are obsessed with individuals. Our articles and books (including this one) are filled with them, which is something you will never find in an article or a book written by an economist. Economists are basically interested in aggregate behaviour that is – somehow – the cumulative outcome of individual decisions and actions. As nicely explained by Thomas Schelling in his classic text, *Micromotives and Macrobehavior* (1978/2006), what economists find fascinating and important is the production of aggregate outcomes, such as the pattern of seating in an auditorium or of ethnic segregation in a housing market, not what is going on in the minds of individuals. If anything, the key psychological question for economists, as exemplified in game theoretic approaches, is precisely how my thinking and behaviour is, or might be, shaped by the thinking and behaviour of the other agents with whom I am interacting at a given moment. For economists, in short, methodological individualism is useful as a way of dealing with the psychological determinants of *collective* life, while *not* having to deal at all with individuals – in which they basically have no interest whatever.

And what about the discipline of psychology? Again, I would say that the charge that it is overly individualistic is misleading, even if it is understandable where this idea comes from. Of course, there are many strands of psychology that, from an anthropologists' point of view, seem weirdly detached from the social realities in which people live. To return to experimental economics, a given task in this field might require participants to divide money with others, but then in the course of the experiment, these people don't actually meet each other. If I'm a participant, I may sit at a computer terminal reacting, on my own, to various scenarios that (hypothetically) involve some other person, who in truth doesn't even exist. Note, however, that even work of this kind is relational, from the psychologists' point of view. That is, the aim is to see how my reactions and moral judgements are influenced by what I think others, even purely hypothetical others, may be doing and/or thinking. In truth, a great deal of psychology is fundamentally relational in this sense, rather than being about the mind-internal thought processes of atomised individuals. (Of course, the methods of psychologists can still be criticised, but I think we should bear in mind that, like the economists, they do have a coherent defence of how they proceed with their empirical and theoretical work.) This is seen in everything from object-relations theory in psychoanalysis to the much more recent experimental research on the psychology of moral judgements – in which a central question is how such judgements are influenced by the presence of third-party observers.

Putting disciplinary particularities aside, it would surely be odd for *any* human scientist (anthropologist, psychologist or economist) to conceive of human psychology as an individual, mind-internal phe-nomenon. It would be odd, first, because as a fundamentally social spe-cies, we are constantly interacting with others. More specifically, we are constantly reading the minds of the people around us, and these other people are constantly reading our minds too. That is, we are engaged in endless cycles of intention-reading and intention-sharing as we go about our lives, a fact that calls our basic 'individuality' into question, and one that surely has major implications for our understanding of economic agency across human societies (Bloch 2013). In particular, as I will discuss later on, the capacity to read and share intentions is what underpins the basic *cooperativeness* of humans, and thus economic life as we experience it in the flow of history.

And then, second, it would be odd to conceive of human psychology as an individual mind-internal phenomenon, because real-world cognition is always profoundly shaped, as I keep suggesting, by cultural-historical artefacts, i.e. by the *collective* products in our cognitive environments that constantly shape our 'individual' thoughts, no matter how private these may appear to be at certain moments. But let me go back to the formulation used at the end of the Introduction. There I said that cultural-historical artefacts *scaffold* individual economic agency in the real world. To be more specific, consider the following:

- These scaffolding effects take place with respect to the *logical*, the *emotional* and the *ethical* aspects of economic agency.

    When people in Angang engage in *logical* deliberation about fishing trips, they draw on a culturally transmitted folk logic that explicitly links risk-taking to family/kinship status (e.g. having grandchildren or not). When in the context of prospective or actual fishing trips they experience *emotional* reactions (e.g. worrying about losing loved ones or feeling a particular dread of drowning), these are shaped in part by rituals of separation and loss that pervade their religious practices and by ghost stories about drowning victims that are widely shared in the local community. In arriving at *ethical* evaluations related to fishing as a way of life, they draw on what they learn from spirit-medium sessions – during which a public discourse about the local moral economy is constantly in the process of being articulated.

- These scaffolding effects take place with respect to *individual* processes of economic agency and also to 'distributed' – i.e. joint or *collective* – ones.

  People in Angang may well (a) think things out logically for themselves, as individuals, (b) experience emotions without sharing these emotions with any other person and/or (c) make private ethical evaluations while sitting in total isolation from the world around them. But as I have explained, decision-making processes surrounding fishing trips to the Philippines – which are simultaneously logical, emotional and ethical – cannot ultimately be understood as 'individual'. They entail complex interactions across networks of persons (across crews, families, the whole community) and are thus always intersubjective and, more properly, *distributed*. Moreover, these decision-making processes depend heavily on the network of cultural-historical artefacts in the surrounding environment – this network itself being part and parcel of the distributed cognition system.

- These scaffolding effects take place with respect to both *micro* and *macro* phenomena, e.g. with respect to one sales transaction but also with respect to the economic history of an entire region.

  In order to understand why individuals in Angang such as Mr Su and Mr Lin take a particular decision – e.g. to go on a dangerous fishing expedition or not – we have to focus not only on what we think they may be thinking but also on the broader social and cultural environment of Angang in which their thoughts are formulated, expressed and acted upon. But the same is true at the macro level. For example, if we want to understand why people in Taiwan have, on aggregate, opted out of particular forms of economic activity (such as small-boat fishing) in favour of others, the cultural-historical artefacts in the environment – definitively including artefacts related to kinship and religion – will have played a central role in this as well.

Taking all of this into account, what I want to argue for in this book is a substantivist economic psychology. This would examine the role that cultural-historical artefacts play in economic agency, as anthropologists would want, but also the specifically psychological mechanisms through which these artefacts have come to exist and to matter in the first place. A substantivist economic psychology approach would, by definition, imply that psychologists have to take seriously into account some of the things that have long interested anthropologists, e.g. the central role that kinship and religion play in economic life in actually existing societies. (As I have already explained, this is not a point about cultural variation, even if the cultural-variation point is itself an important one.) A substantivist economic psychology would also, however, require quite a lot of anthropologists. They would have to pay attention to, and actually grapple with, questions of human psychology rather than seeking to avoid these in the manner of (non-behavioural) economists such as Max Weber.

As part of convincing anthropologists to make a serious effort along these lines, a crucial point I would highlight here is that psychology matters not only at the micro level of small-scale economic decision making but also at the macro level where economic questions become explicitly *political*. As I have explained, most anthropologists would say that the psychology of individual decision making per se is not their interest. That is, the question of whether individual choices – e.g. about what to buy at a given moment – are shaped by cognitive biases *or* by cultural artefacts is largely irrelevant to most of them, most of the time. The contrast between, let's say, the view of a Kahneman (who argues that human thinking, and thus behaviour, is heavily shaped by cognitive biases and dispositions) and a Gigerenzer (who argues that human thinking, and thus behaviour, is heavily shaped by heuristics and other things, including cultural-historical things, to be found in the real-world environments where we live) is not really getting at what, for anthropologists, is the key point – even if their preference would naturally be for Gigerenzer's approach. What anthropologists would really want to stress, vis-à-vis human decision making in the real world, is that the field of choice is always historical. For them, in fact, this is what substantivism is all about: it is a *political* approach in which our psychology (and everything else) is taken as historically determined. But this is precisely why I want to argue for a substantivist economic psychology. For it is equally true that the economic history of humans, with all the politics this implies, has been psychologically determined.

FOUR

Life Plans and Learning

Even the most empirically oriented economists can be said to be ratio-nalists at heart. And whatever else they may be incorporating into their models and analyses these days, it certainly does not include real-world ethnographic stories of the kind that anthropologists generate through participant-observation fieldwork. However, there is at least one impor-tant sense in which economists could be said to be more 'realistic' than anthropologists. They acknowledge that human psychology really *is* at the core of economic agency. Indeed, this helps explain why the behavioural science revolution has had such traction in their discipline in recent years, while being almost entirely ignored by the (empiricist) anthropologists.

Among the economists whose work can be said to have an element of psychological realism to it, while remaining firmly within the rationalist mainstream, is Robert E. Lucas, Jr. In this chapter, as a kind of thought experiment, I am going to place some of Lucas's ideas alongside ethno-graphic material I've collected during fieldwork in rural Taiwan. A good deal of what I say here parallels what has already been said in Chapter 2, where I dealt with everyday decision making in Angang. In other words, there will be a lot of substantivism in which more or less 'everything' (including, once again, kinship and religion) is shown to have economic implications. But there are two points I should make up front about this chapter in particular. First, the underlying focus is not on one-off decisions, per se, but rather on life planning and learning from life – as well as on the consequences of this for the wider economy. In other words, even if the narrative focus remains at the level of individuals and their families, the ultimate questions are more macro in scale, including the question of where the economy as a whole might be headed. Second, whereas in the decision-making chapter I discussed recent contributions to interdisciplinary economic psychology and cognitive science (e.g. the work of Kahneman, Damasio and others), in this chapter I will engage primarily with the work of one influential economist.

I should add that the economist in question is by no means the most obvious person to bring into a dialogue with anthropology. A much more predictable choice, for example, would be someone doing institutional economics, which starts from relatively anthropology-friendly premises.[1] Still, Robert Lucas is about as good a representative as one could hope to find of a particularly influential kind of economics, i.e. the kind that is essentially on a different planet from anthropology. A student of Milton Friedman's, he was awarded the Nobel Prize for his contributions to the rational expectations hypothesis.[2] (For many anthropologists, this is like saying that somebody got a prize for helping spread the plague.) Importantly, one of Lucas's central aims has been to firm up the 'micro-foundations' of his discipline. This has meant grappling, albeit at a highly abstract level, with what are essentially psychological questions.[3] This, in

[1] A Veblen-inspired institutionalism would be much closer to anthropology, but I personally find the stark contrast of a Lucas-like economist with anthropological economics a more thought-provoking comparison. For institutional economics, see Rutherford (2001). On the approach of institutionalists to economic growth in particular, see North (1995).

[2] The Nobel Prize 'advanced information' on Lucas, which neatly summarises his overall contribution to economics, can be found at www.nobelprize.org/prizes/economic-sciences/1995/advanced-information/. For an accessible commentary on Lucas's work on rational expectations, see Schlefer (2012: 199–207).

[3] For thoughtful discussions of the microfoundations literature, see Janssen (1993, 2008). For a paper by Lucas that grapples directly with the relation between psychology and economics, see Lucas (1986).

turn, has led him to take small steps in the direction of psychological realism, e.g. by theorising how *learning* from experience has consequences for the expectations that real-world agents hold about the future. And yet he remains an economists' economist, a strong defender of its fundamentally rationalist orientation. As will be seen, Lucas also has a great deal of faith in capitalism. More specifically, he believes that the capitalist legacy of the Industrial Revolution, which has brought unprecedented wealth to much of the world, will also eventually bring equality.

* * *

In his *Lectures on Economic Growth*, a collection of lectures and essays on endogenous growth theory, Lucas takes on the task of trying to say something general not only about economic growth in the West, but also in the recently developed Asian economies (including Taiwan) and in fact in all of the rest of the world since the Industrial Revolution (Lucas 2002).[4] So far as I know, this stunningly ambitious book has not been read by many anthropologists. One problem is that half of it consists of properly macroeconomic analyses framed in mathematical terms. For example, in a passage where he treats imperialists as monopolists of a kind, Lucas informs us that 'the monopolists' problem is to choose x so as to maximise $f(x) - [f(x) - xf'(x)] - rx'$ (Lucas 2002: 68). And this, I should add, is a really *simple* formula by the normal standards of this author.[5]

By comparison, the other half of the book is very easy to grasp, and I personally find it thought provoking and impressive in different ways. But it does contain a number of passages guaranteed to raise anthropological blood pressures. Lucas coolly observes, for example, that

---

4 Lucas's discussion is partly a critique of neoclassical or 'exogenous' growth theory. See Robert Solow (1997).
5 Fortunately, the introduction to the book provides an accessible overview of its main arguments. See also the very interesting review article by Robert Skidelsky that compares Lucas's book with one by Liah Greenfeld, which basically takes a diametrically opposed (meaning, in this case, very sociologically oriented) view of economic growth (Skidelsky 2003).

'traditional agricultural societies are very like one another, all over the world and over time' (2002: 118). He is also witheringly dismissive of the idea that cataloguing social and cultural differences – in other words, the everyday activity of most anthropologists – will ever help us actually *explain* economic outcomes:

Societies differ in many easily observed ways, and it is easy to identify various economic and cultural particularities and imagine that they are keys to growth performance. For this, as Jacobs (1984) rightly observes, we do not need economic theory: 'Perceptive tourists will do as well'. The role of theory is not to catalogue the obvious, but to help us sort out effects that are crucial, quantitatively, from those that can be set aside. (2002: 30–1)

Ouch. Note, however, that Lucas does *not* claim that social effects, and differences between societies in the course of history, are trivial. On the contrary, his entire analysis is centrally framed around two variables that are surely sociohistorical if they are anything.

The first is 'human capital accumulation', which might just be defined as the process whereby individuals and collectives gain useful knowledge that generates positive economic effects of some kind. It's hard to overstate the significance that Lucas attaches to this particular variable. He says,

The main engine of [economic] growth is the accumulation of human capital – of knowledge – and the main source of differences in living standards among nations is differences in human capital. (2002: 95)

How, then, is this incredibly consequential form of knowledge accumulated? And what exactly *is* it? In his essays, Lucas touches on several distinct knowledge types.[6] First, there are things like technological

---

[6] As Lucas explains, 'Human capital is a broad term, encompassing cognitive achievements that range from basic scientific discoveries to a child's learning how to read or how to plow behind a horse. Which particular activities are we thinking of if we center our view of economic growth and the industrial revolution on human capital

innovations that emerge from specialist (e.g. scientific) programmes of research. That is a kind of human capital. Second, useful innovations might also arise through the direct experience of production. Ordinary workers and their managers who build ships, for example, might learn to handle things more efficiently, thus building more in less time. In this and other illustrations of 'learning by doing', as economists refer to it, an essential point is that 'the production of goods and the production of knowledge are tied together' (Lucas 2002: 14; see also Argote & Epple 1990). Moreover, useful innovations in one firm are routinely distributed as externalities to other firms and industries, including beyond national boundaries. The consequences of this can be very widespread; indeed, they can be global.

As for the third knowledge type discussed by Lucas, this at first glance may seem less explicitly linked to the economy per se than the first two, as well as being harder to capture and quantify. It can just be described as a general level of skill or competence in the population. This might go up with improved education, and for most economists this has indeed been the standard proxy measure for human capital (see further on). But one can imagine it being influenced by many other factors as well, including the gradual spread of ideas of almost any kind around the world. In any case, it is human capital of this third kind – i.e. the more diffuse kind to be found within the general population – to which Lucas ultimately gives priority in his account of economic growth in human history. In order to see why, we must introduce his second key variable, which he refers

accumulation? When Paul Romer stresses "knowledge capital" as "blueprints", he is thinking of human capital at the most abstract and ethereal end of the spectrum: important additions to a society's knowledge that are, for almost all of us, events that happen to us without our doing anything to bring them about. When another economist stresses improvements in literacy, he is thinking of human capital at the other end of the spectrum, far from Science with a capital S, capital that is accumulated only if many people devote their time and energy to doing so. In any actual society, the accumulation of knowledge takes both of these extreme forms, as well as the range of possibilities in between ...' (2002: 159–60).

to as 'the fertility decision'. In brief, Lucas argues that the general rise in human capital (variable 1) is intrinsically linked to the demographic transition in which, over time, the fertility decisions of individuals and collectives (variable 2) have led to much smaller families (2002: 160). Within such families, given the right conditions, investments in human capital can really pay off.

Lucas sums up his general conclusion concerning all of this in relatively straightforward terms, asserting that 'the successful transformation from an economy of traditional agriculture to a modern, growing economy depends crucially on an increase in the rate of accumulation of human capital' (2002: 15–16), something that coincides with an improving rate of return on investments in human capital for most families (2002: 17). What actually leads to this happening, i.e. how family investments in knowledge result in observable economic growth at the macro level, must, of course, be stunningly complex. But as Lucas explains it,

For income growth to occur in a society, a large fraction of people must experience changes in the possible lives they imagine for themselves and their children, and these new visions of possible futures must have enough force to lead them to change the way they behave, the number of children they have, and the hopes they invest in these children. (2002: 17; cf. Easterly 2001: 96–7)

Note that in Lucas's view, this gradual transformation, however complex on the ground, necessarily implies the defeat of traditionalism. People must come to embrace the new, he argues, so as to 'increase the fraction of people in the next generation who can contribute to the invention of new ways of doing things' (2002: 18).

But where is the evidence to back up these claims? Any anthropologist who happened to read this book might find Lucas's approach to reality a bit of a shock – perhaps imagining, wrongly, that economists remain trapped in the type of human science objectivism that went out of fashion in anthropology with the rise of hermeneutics. As Lucas makes clear, however, he is truly a rationalist, exactly the kind of econo-mist I described in the Introduction. His intention, in short, is to apply *pure theory* to the understanding of economic growth, something that necessarily involves

the construction of a mechanical, artificial, world, populated by the inter-acting robots that economics typically studies. (2002: 21)[7]

Of course, rationalist constructs of this type can be tested empirically, and *are* tested by Lucas. But in such testing, as I will discuss at the end of this chapter, it is the aggregate outcomes of things like fertility decisions that matter. Everything else – including the give and take of everyday life – may well be fascinating, but in quantitative terms it is trivial.[8] In fact, when Lucas draws on brief snapshots of 'real life' to illustrate his discussion of learning and economic growth, his source material is the child of the Korean woman who happens to run his laundry in Chicago, characters in a novel by V. S. Naipaul and a *painting* of a traditional farm scene that hangs in his university office.

All of this leads me, an empiricist, to wonder how things 'really' are out there in the world. Lucas (following Jacobs) may be correct to say that the goal of economic theory is not to catalogue the obvious. For me, however, this recalls some advice I heard given by my PhD super-visor, Maurice Bloch. He commented that the task of anthropology is – precisely – to turn the obvious into the problematic. So ...

* * *

During the same year (2000–2001) that I carried out fieldwork in the Chinese community of Protected Mountain (as described at the start of the Introduction), I also lived for a few months in the rural Taiwanese

---

[7] Compare with Solow (1997: 69).

[8] In a fascinating passage (2002: 55–60), Lucas explains why human capital – although seemingly diffuse and unobservable – is 'important in specific, quantitative ways' (2002: 56).

community of South Bridge. Of course, Taiwan is of special interest to economists, including Lucas himself, because of its famously rapid post-war economic growth: it is one of the so-called Four Dragons. And although South Bridge itself may seem an odd location for reflecting on this 'miracle' – it's a relatively sleepy place, and no one there seems especially well off – there are some important parallels, in fact, between Lucas's model and the story of a couple, the Chens, who I came to know well.

Mr Chen was actually born somewhere else, in a large city in another part of Taiwan, where he grew up as one of eight siblings in a poor family. Although he was, he told me, quite a good student, his parents could not afford to keep him in school. As a teenager, and with an introduction from his elder brother, Mr Chen therefore started working in a factory. Most of his workmates had diplomas and seemed to know a lot about everything, or so he felt, and this led him to develop a kind of 'self-loathing' (*zibei*). Having 'looked at himself' (*kan ziji*), he eventually left the factory in order to engage in a process of 'self-learning' (*zixue*). He found sporadic work as an unskilled labourer outside of the factory and, to the grief of his mother, started spending time with some disreputable friends. Then – in his early 20s, and partly in order to escape the influence of these friends – he headed to Taizhong. His mother having passed away, he felt the need to prove to her that he could, after all, make something of himself. Leaving with only NT$50 in his pocket, a farewell gift from his sister, he planned to look for work. But he managed to arrive during the middle of a typhoon and had to survive for two days in the train station with only one steamed bun to eat. On the third day, he secured some temporary construction work, thereby gaining a bit of experience and a few useful connections.

For several years after this, Mr Chen worked on building projects in the Taizhong region. He was later advised to move to the area around his current home, South Bridge, on the grounds that there was a shortage of construction expertise in that particular area. Taking up residence, he shared his knowledge with others while working alongside them. One of his students was an older man who happened to be a respected local spirit medium, and the daughter of this medium eventually became Mr Chen's wife. In time, the new Mrs Chen gave birth to two children, one boy and one girl. But after this she became seriously ill, and all of the couple's accumulated savings went to medical expenses. Mr Chen borrowed heavily and began working double shifts. His father-in-law, as a spirit medium, advised them to seek the assistance of a particular deity, and they did so. Mr Chen made repeated offerings to this deity and pledged that he would become his disciple (*dizi*) if his wife were spared. One day he offered to the god what was meant to be a slow-burning incense roll, which magically flamed up and burnt itself out more or less instantly. Afterwards, Mrs Chen's health began to improve.

During those years, Mr Chen moved between different jobs. He was a construction worker, as I've said, but also a factory worker and a taxi driver, and for a while he also engaged in fishpond cultivation (which is a local specialism). Meanwhile, Mrs Chen worked at a small business she and her husband had established in South Bridge, selling cold teas and shaved ices from an aluminium-roofed stand in the village's small central plaza, in front of the local temple. When I met Mr and Mrs Chen – they were in their fifties at that point – they were concentrating purely on this business. Although the pace of daily life was relaxed, I found that they worked quite steadily, spending something like fourteen hours a day at the stand. Mrs Chen controlled the cash (*guan qian*), she told me, and kept her husband from spending too much on cigarettes and collectable tea sets. They consistently made a small amount of money and managed to save a high proportion of it.

In one of our conversations at the tea stand, the Chens explained to me that they were not especially ambitious. And yet they had, like many people in Taiwan, invested ambitiously in education. In fact, their daughter (who, according to them, was never academically minded) only finished middle school and later began working night shifts with her husband in a nearby factory. However, their son was a very good student who, at the time of my fieldwork, had just finished reading law as an undergraduate at a top university. His mother estimated that they had spent around NT$3,000,000 (something like US$95,000 at the time) on his education. For people like the Chens, this was a stunning amount of money. But their son was filial, and they felt that he fully merited their support. While studying away from home, he was extremely cautious about spending his parents' money even on basic things such as everyday food – a fact that caused Mr Chen's heart to ache (*xinli hen tongku*) whenever he heard of it.

* * *

In certain basic respects, this story fits nicely with a Lucas-like model of economic growth. On the one hand – reckoning things patrilineally – we find a sharp decrease in fertility: eight children in Mr Chen's generation, down to two in his son's. This coincides with a dramatic increase in investments in education. Mr Chen's parents couldn't afford much schooling at all for him, but he could make possible a university degree for his son. Meanwhile, the pattern of knowledge acquisition and distribution found here also (arguably) fits the broad outlines of the Lucas model. Mr Chen went from being an unskilled labourer to being a skilled one. He worked in construction during Taiwan's post-war boom and played a small role in distributing his knowledge of new techniques to other people around him in the countryside. Against a background of rapid economic change, he was prepared to take on new challenges and develop new skills, such as those related to fishpond cultivation. Mr Chen and his wife, as good moderns, gradually shifted, in their modest way, towards working in the service sector, and their son has been prepared for a professional career as a lawyer. Serious prosperity seems to be around the corner. At the time of my fieldwork, the son had a computer, of course, and just about everything else that went along with Taiwanese modernity.

As anthropologists would expect, however, the story of Mr and Mrs Chen has a number of rougher edges to it – that is, once we scale things down to the micro level of ethnographic fieldwork and the everyday experiences of individuals. And in thinking about how best to conceptualise these rough edges, let me start with an important point: that Mr and Mrs Chen are *themselves* economists. They have their own implicit and explicit theories of economic life – ones that, firmly in line with substantivist premises, draw on culturally particular notions of exchange, value, reciprocity and so on, as well as their own direct experience of socioeconomic change. Moreover, Lucas's theory implies precisely an acquired folk economics of this kind. It is not just that people sometimes learn how to do things better. They also learn, as Lucas suggests, to have different ideas about the possibilities in their lives, in part via their interactions with the people around them. Thus it is that they come to revise their economic models. Decisions about crucial things such as fertility and investments in human capital are based, at least in part, on this evolving folk economics. But how does this actually work out in practice? And if Mr and Mrs Chen were themselves asked to comment directly on Lucas's approach, what would they say? What would they ask?

Life Is Fateful

From what I know of the Chens' priorities in life, I suspect that they might start by observing that life is fateful. This could be interpreted in different senses, of course, but it is definitely a non-trivial observation for an economic theory that is framed in relation to the process of *learning from life*. Clear and seemingly predictable patterns of change across a society as a whole may look and feel accidental and unplanned when experienced biographically. This, in turn, is bound to influence what can be *learned* from being caught up in such patterns (which, again, is the key point for present purposes).

Here I should point out at once that the issue of the fatefulness of life has been extensively studied not only by anthropologists but also by a number of economic psychologists and economists, after their fashion. It is seen in economists' debates about risk and 'Knightean uncertainty', a literature to which I will return in a moment. On the anthropology side, we find the work of Mary Douglas and others that focuses specifically on 'risk societies' as well as a much broader literature on the topics of luck, fortune and fatefulness.[9] As one would expect, the anthropologists suggest that in order to understand what problems such as risk or fatefulness imply for ordinary people such as the Chens, we need to understand the particular cultural-historical environments in which they are embedded. This is bound to influence not only their general sense of how life should go, but also will determine the particular conditions under which they make their own decisions about human capital and fertility.

Consider, for example, the fact that Mr Chen's parents did not keep him in school. Why not? I mentioned that he grew up in a relatively poor family. In fact, his paternal grandfather had been a landowner, but it just happened that he (and his wife) died while Mr Chen's father was still young. These deaths, moreover, happened to come during the period of Taiwan's land reform in the 1950s. The timing was extraordinarily bad, Mr Chen told me, because his father – not yet having any idea how to handle such complicated matters – subsequently lost all the family's property. Such bad luck: history can be cruel. As a direct result of these contingent events, which came at a particular moment in Taiwan, his father was unable to invest much in Mr Chen's schooling. It's as if the decision about investments in human capital (here meaning investments by his father in *his* education) were taken for his family by historical happenstance and bad timing, not logical deliberation.

And then there's the fact that Mr Chen's parents had eight children, which undoubtedly made things very difficult for this relatively

---

[9] For a recent intervention in this extensive anthropological literature, see da Col and Humphrey (2012).

poor family. It's impossible for me to know if *this* was planned, but a couple of kinship facts are worth noting. Mr Chen's mother was a 'little daughter-in-law'; i.e. following a relatively common practice of the time, she was adopted as a child by Mr Chen's grandparents to serve as a future wife for their son. As Arthur Wolf has explained, such marriages were undertaken for various (and in fact, one could say, quite logical) reasons.[10] They were not, however, without risks. Such marriages were often unhappy, it seems, and Wolf uses demographic and qualitative data to show in particular that they had above-average rates of adultery and divorce. They also had below-average fertility, especially in cases where the adoption happened during the first three years of the girl's life. (This was as a consequence of an evolved incest aversion, according to Wolf, that made these 'marriages between siblings' inherently problematic.) My point from all of this is simple: although I don't know the age of Mr Chen's mother at adoption, it was almost certainly against the statistical odds for her to have given birth to so many children.

As for the Chens' own generation, they entered into a relatively low-prestige marriage arrangement, one where he did not live alongside his own family (as tradition would dictate). Given the contingencies of Mr Chen's life up to that point, it was far from certain that he was going to even end up in that particular place, South Bridge. But there he did live, and eventually he and his wife – who he just happened to meet and develop a relationship with because her father wanted to learn a trade – had two children. However, this was not the plan. Mrs Chen told me that they would have tried for more, probably something like five, if not for the serious illness she endured as a young mother. Still, given the

---

[10] See Wolf (1995). Many families felt that it was better to have a guaranteed daughter in-law by adopting one (for a relatively low price) when she was still a child than to risk not being able to afford a marriage agreement with a prospective bride's family later on (the latter could be ruinously expensive). It was also widely felt that 'little daughters in law' brought in as children would be more pliable than ones who arrived as adult strangers in their husband's homes following marriage.

current costs of educating children – 'the education problem' (*dushu wenti*), as she refers to it in shorthand – they retrospectively consider this quite a fortunate outcome.

So, looking at the linkages in this case between fertility and investments in human capital – Lucas's core interests – what can we conclude? In brief, Mr Chen's parents might be said to have been *accidentally fertile* (they had eight children, in spite of the fact that his mother was a 'little daughter-in-law'), with the unfortunate result that they could *not* afford to educate their son, Mr Chen. Whereas Mr Chen and his wife might be said to have been *accidentally infertile* (thanks to her illness, they had only two children), with the fortunate result that they *could* afford to educate their son.

As this case study illustrates, but as most of us know from personal experience in any case, life truly is fateful for individuals. Chance events, often largely or entirely out of our control, can have enduring consequences. Of course, at the level macroeconomists such as Lucas worry about, this (mostly) gets ironed out. If over time the fertility rate in Taiwan has gone down, it has gone down – no matter the idiosyncrasies of any family's particular case. If the average level of schooling in Taiwan has gone up over time, it has gone up. Nevertheless, the fatefulness of life does still affect *all* individuals in Taiwan, including those who fall squarely into the average in terms of their life experiences. This implies that fatefulness is *not* irrelevant if we are asking questions about economic psychology, including the question of what agents might *learn* from their (fateful) experiences and thus eventually come to believe, whether individually and collectively, about the future.

One complicating feature is that what we *can* learn from different brushes with fate itself varies. As noted, Mr and Mrs Chen planned to have more children but she then became ill, which meant that it was no longer possible for this to happen. The couple will inevitably have been conscious of this misfortune (her illness) as it unfolded in real time – and presumably learned many things in the course of this. For example, they might have developed a strong belief that a young woman should have children as soon as she reasonably can, rather than leaving it until too late. And they might have subsequently pushed their own daughter to speed things up, even though this would *go against* the clear historical trend in Taiwan towards later marriage and childbirth. Contrast this with the question of what 'fertility lessons' those in previous generations, including Mr Chen's mother, might have learned via the experience of little daughter-in-law marriage. As Arthur Wolf has explained, adults at the time were almost certainly not conscious of the lowered fertility that such marriage arrangements resulted in – something he himself had to figure out through extensive demographic research very long after the fact (1995: 121). Unlike Mrs Chen's awareness of the (unfortunate but obvious) reason why she was not going to have more children, the older generation of Chens simply were not aware of the (unfortunate but non-obvious) fertility deficit caused by that particular type of marriage. Indeed, if they *had* known, little daughter-in-law arrangements wouldn't have been nearly as popular as they were, given that the overriding concern of family elders at the time was to generate offspring. This lack of crucial information caused many families to opt for a 'logical' marriage strategy that was statistically likely to fail – and nor was there any real-time learning opportunity to put them on the right path. So, not only is life fateful, but learning from the fatefulness of life is itself fateful.

This last point may sound overly philosophical, but that has not stopped mainstream economists from considering it in the literature I mentioned above, i.e. the one about risk (a condition in which we can gauge how likely something is to happen) and what is known as Knightean uncertainty (a condition in which we can't do this).[11] In other words, how do individuals – and, more importantly for economists, institutions such as business firms – plan for the future when it involves

[11] Knight (1921); see also Kahneman and Tversky (2000).

factors that are not just unknown but sometimes totally unknow-able? And how does learning play into this? According to Langlois and Cosgel, if we look carefully at the initial contribution to these debates from Frank Knight, his argument is that while agents (as understood for modelling purposes) can in fact 'make subjective probability assess-ments of any situation', there are *some* situations in which their ability to do so is much more constrained – thus creating, for example, problems for insurance markets (Langlois & Cosgel 1993: 457). Notably, then, there is a question of agency at stake in all of this: to what extent, if at all, can we anticipate and thus act in relation to (e.g. insure against) future events? Lucas himself has theorised this problem in relation to expecta-tions of the future (for a relatively accessible version, see Lucas 1977; for a dense mathematical treatment, see Lucas & Prescott 1971). However, the primary goal of economists' work on this topic has of course not been to understand existential dilemmas of the sort encountered by people such as the Chens. It has been, instead, to understand things such as business cycles or the direction of government macroeconomic policy. Moreover – to reiterate the substantivist point – what Lucas and others have concluded about risk/uncertainty is bound to differ significantly from the culturally particular understandings that ordinary people deploy, in real-world settings, as they attempt to navigate their lives.

So, what are these understandings? For the Chens, as with the people from Angang I discussed in Chapter 2, there is an essentially spiritual aspect to the problem of fate. Of course, this does not feature in econo-mists' models. But what I want to stress here is that it actually does affect both (a) how the Chens cognise, and therefore account for, problems related to risk/fate/uncertainty (in whatever sense they might under-stand these terms) and (b) what they learn from particular encounters with risk/fate/uncertainty in the flow of time. Moreover, just as the economists' underlying question could be said to be one of agency, so too – within the folk models – is there a real concern with how much control we have when it comes to problems of fate. As I have explained elsewhere, the basic folk model in rural Taiwan and China holds that (a) life is indeed fateful, and this has to do with cosmological and spiritual processes that to some extent are out of our control and beyond our comprehension; but (b) we can, nevertheless, put a lot of energy into trying to control our own destinies. How can one do this? Divination of the kind discussed in Chapter 2 is one means: this is directed not just at predicting the future but, more importantly, trying to control it to some extent. But there's another way in which one can control fate. This entails making efforts of different kinds (including ritual efforts) to bring the people and/or spirits around us on board – that is, as a means of creating a particular future for our loved ones and ourselves. A key aspect of this, as I will discuss in Chapter 5, is the (difficult) process of cooperating with other humans, especially those with whom our lives are most entangled (Stafford 2007, 2012).

Stepping back, then, one might say that whereas economists have been interested in the extent to which we can predict and thus prepare for what is going to happen next, the people I've met during fieldwork are additionally interested in the extent to which they can change and even *generate* what is going to happen. In any case, here I am simply making a typical anthropological point: that a culturally particular (and 'agentive') understanding of fate is definitely part of the Chens' own economic theory. Moreover, the disjunction between a model of risk/uncertainty as something we respond to and a Chen-like theory of (manipulable) fate should have implications for learning. What we learn from experiences of fate, risk and uncertainty cannot be unrelated to the question of how much control we believe we can have over the course of events. And then one final point, a crucial one in the context of considering Lucas's argument: in Taiwan, a very high proportion of the attempts to manipulate fate (e.g. at spirit-medium altars) relates specifically to fertility (it is about having children and then protecting them) and investments in human capital (a lot of it is about schooling achievement and, more broadly, career-related aspirations).

Smart ≠ Rich

Now let me turn to a second observation that I think the Chens might make. As noted, Mr Chen once tried fishpond cultivation, a business which is known to be high risk (speaking of risk). An entire season's stock can die in a matter of days because of disease or water-quality problems. As a result, a whole science of fishpond cultivation has developed, and as the business has expanded in Taiwan so has the science. The ponds are deeper, aerating machines are used to keep the fish healthy and a range of chemicals are used to improve yields. Some of Mr Chen's friends have remained in the trade, including a man from a nearby village known for his rather analytical approach to everything. However, as Mr Chen put it to me, while this man has a 'good brain' (*tounao hao*), he's never actually succeeded at much in his life. This is because he's a little bit lazy, as the Chens see it, and he also makes errors of judgement in dealing with others. In short, his intelligence, as such, never made him rich. Is it possible that Lucas puts too much faith in the positive consequences of knowledge – that is, of human capital – per se?

In fact, if one turns to the economics literature, similar questions about the link between knowledge and economy have been explored in depth, albeit with reference to very different types of cases, and normally at the macro level. Indeed, there is a long tradition – going back to Adam Smith – both of considering the issue of human capital for economy in general and of unpacking its implications for economic growth in particular (for a useful overview, see Savvides & Stengos 2009). Among many others, the development economist Easterly has summed up some of the data on the relationship between the provision of *education* – which, as noted earlier, is by far the most common proxy measure for human capital – and economic development in a range of countries. Noting the explosion in schooling around the world since 1960, he argues that the measurable economic effects of this have been negligible (2001: 73). More specifically, he finds that the median growth rate of poor countries has actually fallen exactly during a period when these countries underwent a 'massive educational expansion' (2001: 74). Meanwhile, the political economist Amsden (2001), focusing specifically on the case of Taiwan, argues that only certain types of knowledge gains, within certain industries, have led to the remarkable economic growth experienced there. A general level of human capital (or education) within the population as a whole, she suggests, isn't going to get you very far.

But let me go back to the Chens. If forced to say exactly what kind of knowledge you do need in order to participate effectively in economic life, I think they would say that this is a hard question to answer (I'm sure Lucas would concur with this, by the way). In the rural Chinese and Taiwanese folk model of economic success, emphasis is normally given in public discourse to hard work, skill at cultivating connections and good luck, rather than the possession of economic skills and knowledge per se. Obviously, things such as the ability to cultivate useful connections with other people may also be learned; it is also a kind of knowledge or human capital. If we go down that route, however, it starts to become hard to distinguish learning and knowledge that is relevant to economic life from everything else. In the classic terms of substantivism, we face an embeddedness problem in which literally 'everything' might be relevant: i.e. kinship, religion, sociality, etc., all spill over into the economy, and there is no neat boundary at all. Moreover, even where one *can* clearly say that a particular knowledge type (such as computer skills) is having economic effects of some kind, it may be exceedingly difficult to bracket this out neatly for analysis.

Consider the case of numeracy, which I will return to later in the book. Both Mr and Mrs Chen are numerate, and this is obviously a useful type of knowledge for them to possess. It makes it possible for them to calculate prices, make change for customers, do their accounts and so on. But in order to say something empirically meaningful about how they have acquired and make use of numeracy, one would need to study the topic in a lot of detail – and in two very different directions. The development of numerical skills in humans does not start on the job, nor even in school. It begins before birth, i.e. because human infants are born with an evolved neuropsychology that makes numerical thinking possible. Of course, economically useful numeracy takes a long time to develop from this early starting point, and as it does so it will be intensely mediated by such things as school systems and abacuses, i.e. by a range of cultural-historical artefacts to be found in our cognitive environments. Indeed, as I will discuss later on, numerological thinking holds a very special place within Chinese society and culture; that is, it is highly culturally elaborated. All of this means that in Taiwan and China, the acquisition and application of numeracy – which, again, builds on evolved neuropsychology – has to be understood as a social and historical phenomenon too. It is located as much in religious symbolism and cosmology, for example, as it is in schooling or the economy.[12] Needless to say, most economists don't care about this. At most, they might want to know, for example, if the average person in Taiwan is numerate enough to work in an office, shop or factory. But I am simply pointing out that the variable Lucas has introduced into his model – human capital – is ultimately both a psychological and historically constituted one, with all the complications this implies.

Now let me turn to a second 'embedded' knowledge type, this one in the domain of kinship. As with numeracy, knowledge related to family life and kinship has some obvious economic effects – as Lucas's own model incorporates by means of fertility decisions. But this variable is equally difficult to bracket out for analysis. For instance, Mr Chen's awareness of building techniques (an economic skill) arguably turned out to be a kind of 'kinship knowledge' for him. It was integral to his interactions with his future father-in-law, and this gave him the chance to meet his wife. Seen in purely economic terms, this kinship

[12] Among others, see Stafford (2010a).

arrangement – i.e. the marriage to his wife – was initially problematic, as a result of her illness. In the long term, however, it has been of huge benefit. Mrs Chen is a hard-working businesswoman. She keeps a tight rein on the family finances, not least because she knows how to impose her will on her husband. This skill, in turn, requires a kind of knowledge which is probably mostly implicit but which has huge economic effects: the knowledge of how to evoke certain emotional responses in one's relatives to keep them on one's side, to keep them cooperating.

Think of this in terms of parent-child relationships. I've said that it was an accident that the Chens had two children. However, what seems less accidental is that they have been good at raising these children, and in particular have motivated them to make present and future contributions to family security. The bland version of the story is that they were good parents, and the children have been (and are being) good to them in return. However, the actual knowledge which the protagonists mastered and which has informed, among other things, the pattern of their interpersonal relationships, is very subtle. At one point, for example, Mr Chen proudly informed me that his daughter and son had always, even as children, helped out with the family business. After school and during holidays, they would be there at the stand. Interestingly, the son himself told me that this was not true. As a boy, he said, he was treated as a kind of 'child king' (*haizi wang*) because his parents emphasised that he should devote himself entirely to study. As a result, and unlike his sister, he didn't do any work to speak of before the fifth grade. He spent his time 'doing homework'; in other words, as he told me with a laugh, he spent his time messing around with friends. One only has to think about it for a moment to imagine the complexity of what both he and his sister actually learned from this strikingly different treatment by their parents.

These days, in any case, there's no question that both of them are dutiful. Mr Chen said that his son and daughter now actually refuse to allow him to work at all if they are around the stand, claiming that he 'doesn't know how to' (*ta buhui*) serve customers, that he can't make up the various teas they sell, etc. This, however, is not literally true and is in fact a complex statement on the children's part – one that contains both an implicit acknowledgement that it is their time to serve and affectionate mockery for a beloved relative (a crucial component of kinship relations in Taiwan). This attitude has significant economic implications, and it is something which the children must have *learned*. In sum, what I'm describing here is the kind of embedded economic life that anthropologists have always discussed: i.e. it's as much to do with social ties as it is to do with economic rationality or anything else.

But let's try to think of this in the economists' terms. Lucas says that a necessary feature of fast-growth economies is a high rate of return to investing in human capital. If the Chens' son is successful, the investment in him will have been more than worthwhile. However, one's sons can die, or they can turn out to be unfilial, in which case the accumulated investment is rendered useless. These 'anxieties' are built into traditional kinship practices, and they are often expressed in popular culture. What use is a son who hasn't learned to be good to his parents? A related concern focuses on the women one's sons might end up marrying. Mrs Chen explained that nowadays daughters, as much as sons, provide help and support to their parents (as opposed to their husbands' parents) in old age. Her concern is that her son will marry a woman whose parents do not live locally – in other words, that he will do exactly what his father did – as a result of which the new couple will have to divide their attention between two sets of elderly parents (his and hers) living in widely separated places. This would, if you like, harm the rate of return on their investment. As a result, the son is repeatedly instructed by his mother to marry a woman from nearby, so that he will not be too far away when he is needed. But that kind of explicit instruction is relatively superficial. What he really *learns* is something which is difficult to articulate about the nature of his relationship to his parents, and about the emotions of attachment and obligation that he

feels towards them. Within the Chens' own deeply embedded folk economics, the implications of this kind of knowledge are huge, whereas
knowing how to run a small business may not, in the Chens' view, be
such a big or complicated thing. For them personally, moreover, kinship
knowledge is much more important than school-derived knowledge,
notwithstanding the fact that for economists the latter is the proxy measure of human capital, the standard by which the 'useful knowledge' in a
given society can be measured.

Modernisation Is Good for Tradition

I presume that the Chens' first two observations – one concerning
fate, the other concerning the economic effects of particular kinds of
knowledge – would not surprise or trouble Lucas. As I've indicated,
questions about risk and uncertainty, on the one hand, and about the
implications of various types of human capital for the economy, on
the other, have been studied and theorised extensively by economists,
including Lucas himself. One can argue about their conclusions, of
course, and produce an anthropological critique of these conclusions
and the (universalist, ahistorical) models on which they are premised.
But presumably every economist would agree with the Chens that life
is fateful, in various respects, and that the question of whether being
smart, per se, ever really made anybody rich is actually a good one.

However, the third and fourth observations are potentially more
problematic for Lucas's overall account of economic growth in world
history. And the third one is this: that it doesn't really correlate with the
Chens' lived experience to argue that economic growth involves a turning away from tradition. Lucas borrows an evocative phrase from V. S.
Naipaul and suggests that economic growth ultimately requires 'a mil-
lion mutinies' (2002: 18). Along with many other non-anthropological
commentators, then, Lucas assumes that the decline of customary practices is part and parcel of modernisation:

In a successfully developing society, new options continually present themselves and everyone sees examples of people who have responded creatively
to them. Within a generation, those who are bound by tradition can come
to seem quaint, even ridiculous, and they lose their ability to influence their
children by example or to constrain them economically. (2002: 18)

In fact, as the Chens' case illustrates, within the sphere of kinship at
least, this is not what has been happening in Taiwan – and nor is it what
anthropologists have come to expect based on their numerous studies
around the world of the impacts of modernisation and globalisation.[13]
Patterns of kinship in Taiwan (and China) *have*, to be sure, changed
dramatically over the decades in response to evolving political and economic circumstances there (for China, see Yan 2003). Fertility has definitively dropped, so much so that low fertility rather than high fertility is
now the issue of the day; indeed, this is so across the East Asian region
as a whole. But all of these recent changes, and many not so recent ones,
do not imply that the logic of traditional kinship simply withers away.
In fact, many of the processes that might be expected to undermine old
kinship ideologies – for example, the implementation of China's famous
so-called 'one-child policy' – have actually strengthened certain aspects
of them instead (Davis & Harrell 1993).

Very similar points could be made about the fate of religion. I mentioned before that Mrs Chen's father was a local spirit medium. As is
normal with such mediums in Taiwan, there was a small cult around
him – or, to be more exact, around the gods for whom he spoke at his
altar. When he died, it became an obligation for his family to sustain
this cult. This they have done, but it generates certain aggravations.
For one thing, only two of Mrs Chen's five siblings continue to live in
South Bridge. They find it increasingly burdensome to organise the
required rituals, which are quite elaborate and do cost money. The lack

---

[13] Among many other sources on this topic, see Appadurai (1996), Fuller (2004) and
Inda and Rosaldo (2008).

of enthusiasm is palpable, and from this little snapshot we might imagine that Taiwanese popular religion – at least of the classic kind that was
practised in the past by Mrs Chen's father – is now in a process of decline.
Who wants to keep it going? In fact, while it can certainly be said that
religious practice in Taiwan is changing, there is little evidence of any
decline. A key point is that enduring prosperity – the consequence of the
'miracle' – has actually made it much easier for communities to build
temples and to underwrite elaborate celebrations for the gods. Indeed,
I would emphasise that people in rural Taiwan explicitly link worship
of this kind to prosperity: in the local/folk model, economic growth is
precisely due to the strength of communal ties to 'effective' (*ling*) gods.
It is hardly surprising, then, that modernisation has been very good for
the religion business.[14]

But things do of course change, and the Chens' own personal religious preferences have evolved in a somewhat different direction from
those of older generations. Like many people in Taiwan, they have
become involved in new religious movements that bring together, and
transform, traditional elements from Buddhism and Daoism. These are
movements that in general might be called less militaristic (in terms of
the style/aesthetics of ritual practices) and less competitive (in terms of
the sectarian tensions between cults and between communities) than
classic Taiwanese local religion as well as more focused on spiritual
development and universalistic good works. Among other things, they
often travel outside of South Bridge to worship with other members of
their group – which is explicitly defined neither by locality nor by kinship. This is a big change, a really important one.

---

[14] One thing I found especially striking during my fieldwork in South Bridge was the
extent to which young men in the countryside were keen religious participants.
They were not so much interested in the boring everyday routine of worshipping
in temples and studying doctrines, but rather in rowdy spirit-possession episodes
and in the militaristic performances which accompany the sacred images of gods on
pilgrimages between temples. For them, the traditions of Taiwanese local religion are
very far from dead.

But what about their son? During my fieldwork, he was away from South Bridge much of the time, and thus I did not talk directly with him about his religious beliefs and practices. But he is certainly dutiful when it comes to the basic requirements of Confucian propriety. With regard to this, his father told me that his son's time at university had been really useful in one way. As I said earlier, Mr Chen moved away from his own family at an early age, and he later lived uxorilocally – i.e. with his wife's kin rather than his own – which is a non-traditional arrangement. Still, he always felt obliged to worship his family's ancestors, especially at the times of year when such worship is more or less mandatory. This has never been especially convenient for him. However, his son (luckily) ended up at a university where he could easily worship the family ancestors. This he did without fail, at the correct time, without even having to be reminded to do it by his parents, according to Mr Chen. Moreover, at the time of my fieldwork, one could well imagine that in the future he would live near his parents, as they clearly wanted him to do, and that when his father dies he will be totally proper vis-à-vis the ongoing rites and remembrances for him. In short, Mr Chen's son is being lined up to be *much* more traditional – in terms of the classic demands of Chinese kinship in general, and in relation to ancestral worship in particular – than Mr Chen himself ever was. One can hardly claim that he is learning to give up the ways of the past.

The Value of Your Investments Can Go Down as Well as Up

The topic of the ancestors takes me to the Chens' fourth and final observation, which relates to history and to Lucas's generally optimistic take on global economic prospects. This is not something on which I focused in my summary of his argument, but it really does underpin the whole book. Lucas asks, will the economic success of the West, recently exported to certain places in Asia, such as Taiwan, be exported eventually to everywhere else? And his answer is yes. The knowledge that is there in Western economies – and the practices derived from this knowledge – has been filtering outwards to all countries, thus ironing out lingering problems elsewhere. He points out that rough *equality* of incomes across the world has been the norm for most of human history; i.e. we have all been equally poor together. The Industrial Revolution, however, brought an anomaly: huge growth in some places, which led to unprecedented variations in wealth. In the twenty-first century, he says, equality – the norm predicted by economic models – will start to reassert itself.

The legacy of economic growth that we have inherited from the Industrial Revolution is an irreversible gain to humanity, of a magnitude that is still unknown. It is becoming increasingly clear, I think, that the legacy of inequality, the concomitant of this gain, is a historical transient (Lucas 174–5).

Needless to say, this does not coincide with what Piketty (2014) and others have argued, more recently, about the general direction of travel when it comes to patterns of inequality in the world.[15] Even ignoring the Piketty challenge, however, it's hard to know how to respond as an anthropologist to an argument of the kind that Lucas puts forward here – which is not only posed at a global scale but also based on a range of aggregative statistics that are very remote from the level of everyday · lived experience we witness during fieldwork. Given the intrinsically radical stance of most anthropologists, Lucas's faith in capitalism and markets is bound to seem, for them, not only scientifically misguided[16] but also morally objectionable.

And yet, of course, Taiwan *is* a special case when it comes to the (apparent) benefits of capitalism. There's a whole story to be told about Taiwan's gradual transformation in the post-war decades and about the

---

[15] For a very thought-provoking commentary on the impact of Piketty's work, see Wade (2014).

[16] For a brief, and highly critical, snapshot of Lucas's 'new classical macroeconomics', see Kurz (2016: 146–8).

(highly contentious) role played by the ruling KMT in this transformation. During the years of high Maoism on the mainland, however, Taiwan massively out-performed China on the economic front – and was actually a relatively egalitarian society, as a result of comprehensive land reform and other measures that followed the end of Japanese colonial rule. More than forty years after China's economic reforms were launched, Taiwan's per capita GDP is still around 2.5 times great than that of China. People in Taiwan are very conscious of this, of course – how could they not be?

Still, I think the Chens would be cautious about the idea that prosperity is here to stay. There could be both personal and collective (while still local) reasons for this. At a personal level, it's hard for Mr Chen not to remember, for example, that his grandfather – the landowner – happened to die in the middle of Taiwan's land reform, thus depriving him of schooling (as Mr Chen now understands things). The same kind of fatefulness can be said to bedevil local, national or regional economies as well; i.e. the wrong things can happen at the wrong time. In fact, all of the communities in which I have conducted fieldwork have lived through dramatic shifts of fortune due to events largely beyond their control. As I explained at the start of the Introduction, this is very striking in the case of Protected Mountain (in south-west China): the signs of decay from an earlier period of relative grandeur, which predated Maoism, are everywhere one looks. The modern economic history of South Bridge is less dramatic but nonetheless volatile. When Mrs Chen was a girl, before her husband arrived on the scene from outside, she did backbreaking work in the salt fields around South Bridge. But the local economy of salt production eventually collapsed because of cheaper production outside of Taiwan, and successive prospects for local people have gone or are going the same way. According to Mr Chen, ten or twenty years ago things were actually looking good in this place, partly because there were factories in the region where young people could work. This is no longer true, because much of Taiwanese manufacturing has moved in recent decades to China and other countries. For a period, he said, Taiwan was awash with money earned on the stock markets, but then the markets collapsed and the crisis in the Asian economies caused a general slump in consumption of iced teas and everything else. Although some local people still engage in fishing or small trading, many rely on remittances from their children, on public-sector employment or on handouts of various kinds to get by. As a result, South Bridge feels, on the whole, like a sleepy place, and it is probably not a very good illustration of Taiwan's prosperity.

In case you were worried, the economists do have an explanation (probably many explanations) for this. As Easterly and others have pointed out, economic development always entails some people losing out, some of the time. In Taiwan as elsewhere, 'creative destruction' is simply part of the game (Easterly 2001: 171–93). It is the destiny of the sleepy outposts, and of tradition-bound cultural conservatives, to be left behind. But one cause of the current sleepiness of South Bridge has had an especially direct impact on the Chen family. Briefly, the community is not far from a pilgrimage destination. Much of the success of their business was due to the steady stream of pilgrims who went straight past the temple in South Bridge, and past their tea stand, en route to the final (and bigger) destination up the road. Several years ago, however, a fateful decision was taken. The road to the pilgrimage centre was going to be improved and widened, and it could either go through South Bridge (in which case some houses would have to be knocked down) or a bypass (as good an illustration as any of 'creative destruction') would have to be built. After much discussion, the bypass was built, and Mr and Mrs Chen saw a steep decline in their trade.

Concerning this sequence of events, however, they are philosophical. With their son having completed his studies, with their house paid for and with savings in the bank, they don't need extra income. They are happy and dedicate quite a bit of their time (and a significant part of their money) to religious activities. On many evenings, they also sit under electric lights at a table in their tea stand, in the middle of the darkened temple plaza, performing a kind of labour which played a big role in Taiwan's original economic expansion: they do piecework on little plastic trinkets such as keychains and children's toys, which they said are exported to America. As Mr Chen explained to me, this kind of work is exactly what made Taiwan prosperous in the first place, because it is very efficient. If somebody has to build a factory, he said, it costs too much, and then you have to pay taxes and insurance, and then you have to pay more and more wages, and then you have to sort out retirement plans for your employees. When all of this is done, how can you possibly compete with factories in countries where such things are not required? It's as if people get too smart and demanding in terms of what they want from working – and then you go into decline. But he told me that if things get bad, the Taiwanese people will not be afraid to turn to things like piecework on trinkets in their own homes again.

In fact, the immediate reason for this work is a bit more complicated. As Mrs Chen's brother (Mr Chen's brother-in-law) explained things to me, women from Taiwan are now disinclined to marry a Taiwanese man unless he has a good education, a good job and a good car. Having none of these things, he has therefore married a Vietnamese woman of Chinese descent, and he and his wife and their baby son now live in South Bridge with his mother, near the Chens. Since his Vietnamese wife is unable to work outside of the village, she does piecework in order to be able to send small remittances back to her family. Everybody helps her out with this work, sitting at the Chen's tea stand under the electric lights, when there's nothing more pressing to do, thereby doing their part for economic growth in … Vietnam.

* * *

I've briefly outlined four – highly general – observations that I believe Mr and Mrs Chen might make about Robert Lucas's book, if they were to read it. Now let me reiterate these but also state them a bit more systematically, in the form of questions:

- What are the implications of the fatefulness of life for a theory of economic growth that takes learning and knowledge, investments in human capital and fertility decisions as key variables? This question could be interpreted as a universalist one – that is, because people in *all* societies must deal with fate, risk and uncertainty, not least when it comes to fertility decisions within families. But it is also a question about cultural variation – that is, because the cultural-historical artefacts that surround fate/risk/uncertainty vary hugely, with implications for how real people in real societies actually learn and think and decide as economic life progresses. Among other things, these artefacts will shape the extent to which people believe they can actually intervene in matters of fate.
- Given that human capital (knowledge) is embedded in and influenced by 'everything' (from the evolved neuropsychology of numeracy to the intense emotions that pervade everyday family life), how can one bracket it out for analysis, and claim that having *more* of it will have intrinsically positive effects? Can it be right that the level of education, per se, can be taken as the useful proxy for human capital? To state the obvious, an important point is that the economic usefulness of any given knowledge type (including advanced education) will depend on historical context: it isn't a static variable.
- Given the cumulative anthropological evidence (and certainly not only from South Bridge) that processes of modernisation/ globalisation can actually be rather good for tradition, and can even rest significantly on traditional underpinnings, why argue the opposite? Notably, there are many people in Taiwan who would claim that economic success there has been a direct gift from the gods, and by extension a product of human worship of these gods. And it is definitely the case that economic success has underwritten massive

investments in Taiwanese religious practices, including at the local level (something, by the way, that is now being exported to China).

- Given the volatile history of places like South Bridge, something that influences the folk economic models of people there, why the optimism about global economic prospects? Why the teleology? Of course, one can say that the macro evidence points in one historical direction only: towards global capitalism and an equitable distribution of wealth. But from a folk point of view, this might seem more a matter of faith than of certainty. Just as fatefulness intervenes in the life of one family, so it can and does intervene in national and global history.

As I've already remarked, I suppose that the first and second observations would not trouble Lucas. He understands that life is fateful in various senses and has actually written on this topic. He also knows there's an interesting question to be asked about the economic usefulness of different knowledge types (types of human capital) at particular historical moments. As for the third observation, my best guess is that Lucas would probably bat this aside. It may be true that some aspects of tradition survive the transition to modernity, and even thrive under it, but on the whole one can say that the world has been radically transformed and that there will never be any going back on this. As for the fourth observation, I presume that his fundamental opinion about the consequences of the Industrial Revolution and capitalism for the direction of human history would be unlikely to be changed by a few fieldwork stories about one family in rural Taiwan.

Actually, Lucas might also point out that anthropologists – and the people such as the Chens about whom they write – do not have a monopoly on storytelling. Here is one of his own characterisations of what economists aim to do in their work: 'We are storytellers, operating much of the time in the worlds of make believe.' But he then goes on to add what is, for an economist, the crucial point:

We do not find that the realm of imagination and ideas is an alternative to, or retreat from, practical reality. On the contrary, it is the only way we have found to think seriously about reality. (Lucas 2011)

Beyond this strong defence of rationalism – which could also, of course, be read as an attack on pure empiricism of the kind that anthropologists practise – Lucas might remind us that even the most rationalist of economists believe in reality checks. A clear illustration of this is found in an earlier paper by Lucas, also on economic growth, in which there is a chart showing (actual) annual rates of growth for a number of Latin American countries (Lucas 1986).[17] These growth rates match strikingly well what a particular macroeconomic model would predict, and near the end of his paper Lucas thus returns to discuss the chart as follows:

Each 'point' in [the chart] represents the behavior over a period of 20 years of all the individual households and business firms in a single Latin American country. To a sociologist or an anthropologist, these 16 countries exhibit an enormous variety of quite different cultures. To a political scientist, they cover a range from liberal democracy through military dictatorship. To a psychologist, they consist of millions of individual personalities, with most of those alive at the end of the period not yet born at its beginning. To an economist, they are 16 points lying (more or less) on a theoretically predicted 45-degree line.

To observe that economics is based on a superficial view of individual and social behaviour does not, in these circumstances, seem to me to be much of an insight. I think it is exactly this superficiality that gives economics much of the power that it has: its ability to predict human behaviour without knowing very much about the makeup and the lives of the people whose behaviour we are trying to understand. (1986: S425)

---

[17] Lucas's 2002 book is also filled with empirical information related to the models he is trying to develop. For example, see his extensive discussion of the Penn World Table project (2002: 114 ff).

For an economist of the Lucas type, the key phrase in the passage I have just cited is 'theoretically predicted'. This nicely sums up the desired relationship between (unreal) macroeconomic modelling and the (real) world out there in which we live. Of course, one of the main criticisms the economists have faced is that they *cannot*, in truth, predict anything at all with accuracy.[18] Still, I suppose a critic of anthropology might point out that we describe more or less everything while explaining (or even trying to explain) very little. My own view is that anthropologists should show some intellectual generosity towards other human scientists who are treading a very different path from our own. In the end, I disagree with Lucas about many things, and perhaps especially when it comes to the things that matter most. I definitely have much less faith in capitalism than he does. But I do find impressive the seriousness of his questions and his methods. To be more specific, one thing I find especially impressive is his attempt to grapple with the implications of *learning* for folk economic understandings – and his attempt to incorporate this learning phenomenon into his (highly abstract) macroeconomic models. In the paper on growth rates in Latin America that I have just referred to, Lucas comments as well that the predictive power economists aim for 'necessarily has its limits'; and indeed the whole point of that paper, and one could say of Lucas's work as a whole, is precisely to try to transcend these limits by a little bit, thus improving macroeconomics, however incrementally (Lucas 1986: S425). In other words, he is constantly trying – slowly, carefully – to make his theories better. This is something that anthropology could learn from.

---

[18] For a concise summing-up of the dangers of an economics which, on the one hand, wants to be treated as a science and yet has no predictive powers, see Rosenberg and Curtain (2013). They suggest that 'economics has never been able to show the record of improvement in predictive successes that physical science has shown through its use of harmless idealizations. In fact, when it comes to economic theory's track record, there isn't much predictive success to speak of at all.'

FIVE

Self-Education as the End of Economic Life

Once we start asking questions about the psychology of economic life, we will naturally be led to ask some questions about *learning*, as Robert Lucas and a number of other economists have done in recent years. We ought to bear in mind, however, that economy is correlated with learning in two very different, if sometimes overlapping, senses. On the one hand, in order to be competent economic agents, we should have (already) learned certain things. A farmer, for example, is someone who knows how to farm. On the other hand, economic life is *itself* educational. A farmer may acquire new knowledge and skills, and perhaps even wisdom, as things progress. In this chapter, my primary focus is going to be on this second kind of learning, i.e. the kind that comes to us from economic agency. And my conclusion, to anticipate, will be that the single most important thing we learn about in this way is ourselves. More specifically, through a difficult process of 'self-education', we learn about the cooperative species essence that is shared by all humans.

In what follows, I am going to explain what I mean by this and also illustrate it with a real-world case study drawn from fieldwork in northeast China. First, however, I need to situate my discussion with respect to the broader ambition for this book, i.e. to my attempt to bring anthropology, psychology and economics into some kind of conversation. In aid of this, I will start with a brief philosophical detour, one in which the underlying approaches of Utilitarianism and Marxism to questions of economic psychology will be compared. These two traditions have been central to the disciplinary histories of economics and anthropology, respectively, and are typically understood to be totally opposed to each other. Both traditions have also been the subject of endless debate over the years, a good deal of it impenetrable to non-specialists. But here I will aim to simplify matters for readers in two ways. First, I am going to use plain, ordinary language in my discussion – so that even if you're not always sure what Hegel (for example) is talking about, you should always at least know what I'm talking about. Second, so as not to get bogged down in interpretive arguments, I will largely present Marxism and Utilitarianism as ideal types, based on my own understandings. As will be seen, my ideal type of Marxism is influenced by the philosopher Allen Wood. In brief, Wood convincingly shows (a) that Marx needs to be understood in the context of the German philosophical tradition from which he emerged and (b) that many of the things we tend to associate with Marx – such as him being anti-Utilitarian – deserve rethinking. My ideal type of Utilitarianism is influenced, in turn, by the philosopher Derek Parfit. In brief, Parfit convincingly shows (a) that Utilitarianism is a subtler, and potentially more radical, philosophy than most anthropologists assume and (b) that many of the things we tend to associate with Utilitarianism – including its presumed opposition to other approaches, including Kantian deontology – deserve rethinking.

* * *

So, let me start, then, with Utilitarianism – which anthropologists usually dismiss out of hand as a bogus, even malevolent, philosophy because of its presumed link to the discipline of economics, to rational-choice theory and to unrestrained capitalism. In other words, for them this philosophy is the starting point for an *amoral* approach to economy in which everything we do is reduced to self-interested calculation. Is this a fair reading? Or is it based on a caricature of what Bentham, J. S. Mill and others actually wrote and felt? Bart Schultz has recently suggested that, in truth, Utilitarianism is 'more accurately charged with being too demanding ethically than with being too accommodating of narrow practicality, material interests, self-interestedness and the like' (Schultz 2017: 3).[1] Certainly, the early Utilitarians (and also Adam Smith, whose relationship to Utilitarianism is much debated) believed that they were engaged in developing a *moral* science of economy – one that could, moreover, help us improve the world in which we live. Of course, the subsequent history of economics can be told as a shift *away* from this explicitly philosophical and normative starting point. However, its legacy is nevertheless obvious today, if one looks for it.

But allow me to take a step back in order to explain. Utilitarianism, which in common with all philosophies comes in competing versions, is the most famous type of Consequentialism. What this means is that it focuses our attention on the consequences or outcomes of our decisions, actions, social arrangements, etc. With regard to morality, for example, a Utilitarian would argue that the best way for us to be good is not to follow a priori principles but rather to reflect on the good or bad outcomes that our decisions and actions lead to. The same holds true collectively. The best economic system for a people to adopt – the morally preferable system – would be the one most likely to generate the best overall consequences, something measurable in terms of wealth, happiness or some other 'utility'. If the starting point for this collectively beneficial outcome is a form of self-interest, so be it.

Notwithstanding Utilitarianism's bad reputation among anthropologists – and leaving aside its influence within economics – it should be noted that Consequentialism as a whole remains one of the three central strands of contemporary moral philosophy. In other

---

[1] See Kurz (2016): 17–41. For an interesting discussion of ethics and economics which considers Utilitarianism alongside deontological ethics and virtue ethics, also see van Staveren (2007).

words, philosophers take it very seriously. Moreover, Utilitarianism/ Consequentialism can accommodate a wide range of views. Notably, Derek Parfit, the greatest of modern Consequentialists, was centrally concerned with questions of the kind that anthropologists themselves have sought to pursue – in 'anti-Utilitarian' mode, as they would understand this. To be more specific, Parfit has asked probing questions about (a) the assumptions made by economists and others about the reasons we have for acting in particular ways and (b) the outcomes that we should be aiming for when it comes to our collective social and economic life. Any anthropologist who thinks of Utilitarianism as a useless (or, worse, positively dangerous) philosophy should read Parfit's thought-provoking reflections on 'what matters' (Parfit 1984, 2011).

In any case, the thing I want to highlight here is that Utilitarians,[2] in line with their focus on consequences, generally take the economy as a means to (good) ends, however defined, rather than it being an end in itself. And the specifically *psychological* questions that therefore come into focus for them – and this is clearly so if one fast-forwards from classic Utilitarianism to recent approaches in economic psychology – are to do with the 'before' and 'after' of economic agency rather than the 'during'.[3] More specifically, the central questions are to do with

---

[2] In what follows, as will be seen, I am primarily concerned with psychologists and economists who could be said to have a 'Utilitarian' orientation, by way of contrast with Consequentialist philosophers, including the classic Utilitarians.

[3] This is not to say that the 'during' is ignored by Utilitarians and/or economists. As I will discuss in a moment, Adam Smith, John Stuart Mill and others saw economic activity *itself* as morally important, and saw the way in which we organise our societies, be it for economic or any other purpose, as having deep moral implications. Also on the question of the 'during', note that modern economists have explored the economic consequences of what they call 'learning by doing', e.g. on factory floors. Note, however, that the focus in such research is explicitly on what this form of learning implies for economic outcomes, not on learning via economic agency as a worthwhile end in itself.

- the consequence-producing psychology that we *bring* to economic agency and that shapes our economic decisions and behaviours, e.g. the disposition to be selfish as opposed to fair in transactions with others.
- the extent to which what *follows* from economic decisions and behaviours actually does succeed (or not) in making us happy, satisfied, etc., assuming these are the desired consequences.

Both sides of this equation have been subject to empirical study on a grand scale in recent years. As explained in the Introduction, the psychology we *bring* to economic agency has been explored extensively by experimental economists and others. One core finding, put simply, is that on average we bring a broadly 'cooperative' mindset to economic transactions. That is, we are prepared to incur costs to the benefit of others even when – according to the rules of a particular game – we could actually get away with being very (or entirely) selfish. Moreover, the disposition to 'cooperate' in this particular sense – i.e. to be moral economic agents rather than purely selfish ones – is not something we have to learn through experience; it is just how we are (thus the obvious anthropological critique that research along these lines ignores the role that cultural learning and history play in shaping the values, preferences and behaviours of real-world economic agents).

Meanwhile, the psychology that *follows* from economic life has also been explored extensively. The headline finding here, put simply, is that material wealth per se does not make people happy or sustain well-being. What *does* make them happy is harder to characterise in simple terms. However, living in broadly 'cooperative' (in effect, morally coherent rather than atomistic) social settings appears to help, as one might expect. The neo-Utilitarian economist Richard Layard has spelled this out in more detail, suggesting (and the particulars are intensely debated in this field, understandably) that variation in happiness can broadly be explained by the presence or absence of six key variables – most or all of which can be related back, in the terms I am using here, to life in a 'cooperative' social context. These variables are the presence or absence of strong and stable families, solid communities and friendships, secure employment and income, good health, personal freedoms (including vis-à-vis government) and adherence to systems of morality such as religion (Layard 2005: 70–1).[4]

It is no accident that so much work has been done, and is still being done, on the psychological before and after of economic life. As explained, even the most model-oriented of rationalist economists take it for granted that human psychology really *is* at the heart of economic agency. Moreover, Utilitarian approaches clearly lend themselves to a psychological reading and more specifically to a focus on decision making and its psychological consequences: as it were, the input side and the output side of economy. When I refer to the continuing influence of Utilitarianism in today's supposedly 'unreal' economics, notwithstanding the discipline's shift away from its normative and philosophical starting point, this is a key place where it is found. That is, it is found in a research focus on *consequential decisions* and how these should be understood – or at least dealt with analytically for the sake of modelling.

Still, the recent empirical findings could be said to make uncomfortable reading for at least *some* economists. In short, the evidence does not add up to a ringing endorsement either of (a) self-interested rationality as an account of how people think and arrive at decisions or of (b) unrestrained capitalism and wealth acquisition as an account of how people ought to live. In other words, we are not rational maximisers of utility, in any simple sense, and nor does the pursuit of wealth appear to make us happy, in any simple sense.

Note, however, that a Consequentialist in the Parfit mould might really welcome such findings, just *because* they force us to think more deeply about what matters in our collective social and economic life.

---

[4] There is now a huge literature in the economics of happiness and well-being, and a great deal of ongoing research and debate. For an anthropological discussion of happiness in China, see Stafford (2015) – as well as the broader anthropological discussion/critique of this research topic by Walker and Kavedzya (2015).

Meanwhile, the neo-Utilitarian economist Richard Layard, whose work I have just cited, has positively embraced the findings and explored their policy implications in detail. He argues, among other things, that in order to increase social well-being overall, we should impose significantly higher taxes – thereby funding social programmes specifically designed to tackle misery head-on (Layard 2005). Indeed, a social interventionist approach of this kind – which is not without its critics[5] – could even be interpreted as a Utilitarian step in the direction of serious economic redistribution, one might even suggest of Marxism.

* * *

At first glance, however, the Marxist take on all of this seems radically different from the Utilitarian one. Marx famously stressed the intrinsically political nature of economy, highlighting the exploitative nature of capitalism in particular. Economy is not, after all, a domain of decision making and its psychological consequences, but rather one of mass coercion. To put this differently, if Utilitarian economic psychologists have been impressed by how cooperative humans turn out to be in the context of market transactions with strangers, Marx is unimpressed by the larger system within which the apparent fairness of exchange actually hides a deeper fraud.

And yet the gap between Marxism and Utilitarianism is not so great as might be assumed. I will return to this more fully later, but here let me simply note that Marx's *political* theory has two interconnected *psychological* points at its core – ones that arguably add to, rather than contradict, Utilitarian understandings of the economic psychology of humans.[6] First, he tells us that capitalism rests to a great extent on a failure of learning. The exploited (however cooperative their intentions may

---

[5] For a critique of this approach, see Davies (2011).
[6] As I will discuss further on, it seems to me that the recent findings in economic psychology, as well as in cognitive science more broadly, about human 'cooperativeness' would be very much welcomed by Marx. The question would be how such (empirical) findings fit with his view of the *political* nature of economy and with his theory of the ideology that underpins capitalist relations of production.

be) do not fully grasp the conditions in which they live; thus the theory of ideology. Second – and this may be read as a more philosophical version of the first point, but it is no less political for that – he tells us that capitalism impedes human self-realisation; thus the theory of alienation.

The meaning of this second point, much debated over the years, can be glossed as follows: through productive labour and through social relations directed at meeting their needs, humans are in a position to realise, externalise and/or actualise themselves as humans in a deep sense – more specifically, to realise/externalise/actualise their cooperative *species essence*. But this is just exactly the thing that capitalism obstructs, according to Marx. It alienates products of labour from those who make them and more generally distorts cooperative relations of production, reproduction and exchange between individuals. In effect, it detaches us from each other and thus from our essentially cooperative nature as humans. As a result, capitalism is not only exploitative but in a more fundamental sense actually debilitating.

However, what this typical gloss of Marx's ideas about alienation fails to make explicit enough, in my view, is its specifically *cognitive* dimension – i.e. exactly the thing that brings the theories of ideology and alienation together. Indeed, this cognitive dimension of his work is routinely elided in commentaries on Marx in spite of its obvious centrality to the philosophical tradition from which he emerged. As understood within this (German idealist) tradition, achieving self-realisation means simultaneously becoming oneself and coming to *know* oneself through an active process of 'self-education' (*selbst-bildung*). Allen Wood is here a useful guide. As he explains, at the core of Hegel's anthropology – which deeply influenced Marx's anthropology – we find the German notion of *bildung*, i.e. learning, education or culture. In short, Hegel argues that meaningful human learning is always *self*-education, which is to say that it

occurs not primarily through the imparting of information by a teacher, but instead through what [Hegel] calls 'experience': a conflict-ridden process in the course of which a spiritual being *discovers* its own identity or selfhood while striving to *actualize* the selfhood it is in the process of discovering. (Wood 1998: 301, emphasis added)

Admittedly, the Hegelian language of spiritual discovery in this argument may not sound very Marxist at all to most readers. Marx, as they say, turned Hegel's *idealism* on its head – which is presumably the reason that the cognitive dimension of his work is elided in most commentaries on him today. Nevertheless, Hegel's notion of self-education as the outcome of a conflict-ridden process of learning definitively remains at Marxism's core (see Wood 2004 [1981], Kolakowski 2005 [1978]). Moreover, this learning process is conceived by Marx (as it was by Hegel and Fichte before him) as intrinsically tied to 'economic agency' under a very broad definition, as I will explain more fully later. In short, it is through our active engagement with, and struggle against, both nature and other humans, in the course of meeting our needs, that we come to learn about ourselves.

To state this schematically, then,

- for humans, to *become* oneself and to *know* oneself are always two sides of the same coin;
- this dual process of becoming and knowing is always *active*: it goes beyond contemplation and is framed in particular around transforming the world, oneself and others through activity;
- it is always *relational*: the 'self' of becoming and knowing is caught up in (transformative) social ties; and
- it is always *historical*: self-education occurs within particular historical moments.

* * *

I'll return to the question of human self-education in a moment. At this point, however, let me briefly recapitulate what I have said thus far, making a few additional points. Utilitarians (at least, my ideal type version of them) are interested in the psychological inputs and outputs of economic agency, including the decisions we make and how we feel about the consequences these lead to. Recent evidence suggests that we are broadly 'cooperative' on both sides of this before/after equation, as opposed to entirely selfish. Marxists, for their part, are interested in a very different, and yet not unrelated, kind of economic psychology: in the contribution that economic agency itself might make – if it is not distorted by the twin problems of ideology and alienation – to human self-education, i.e. to us *knowing* ourselves, a process intrinsically tied to us *being* ourselves, to us being essentially human.

For Utilitarians, a good outcome from economic life as a whole (and this is hardly a foolish thing to wish for) would be one in which people on aggregate are happy, satisfied, etc., and more broadly one in which 'things go well' for them in an important sense.[7] The evidence seems to suggest that this would be more likely to occur within an essentially cooperative form of life, as opposed to an atomistic/individualistic/ selfish one. Surely a Marxist would also find widely distributed happiness and well-being a desirable consequence, would want things to 'go well' for people in an important sense and would agree that this would be more likely to occur within an essentially cooperative form of life. Note, however, that if happiness implies an absence of struggle, it might also imply a reduction in chances for learning.[8] And this is an important consideration. In short, the psychology that Marxism cares about, in the end, is not the (output) psychology of well-being but rather the (processual) psychology of self-education. For it is through the conflict-ridden, and thus intrinsically *difficult*, process of learning

---

[7] Note that, at least in the normal telling, this would be an indirect rather than direct outcome of economic activity. For example, one could say that it isn't economic activity per se that makes us happy, but rather the security that comes from economic activity.

[8] The point about struggle as the prerequisite for learning is summarised nicely in relation to Hegel (and his famous master-slave dialect) in Wood (2014: 224–5).

through economic agency that we have the potential both to grasp how we live and how to change it. But learning about what?

* * *

In shifting the focus to the real world, let me start with four very general points before getting to more detail. The first is that many of the people I happen to have met during my periods of fieldwork in rural Taiwan and China do not actually spend a great deal of time working.[9] They sometimes work extremely hard, to be sure, but then many of them have significant periods of *not* working at all. For example, the fishermen I met in Taiwan in the 1980s were kept at home many weeks of the year by bad weather, by the natural cycles of fishing and by regulations that restricted time at sea. The farmers I met in northeast China a few years later, in the early 1990s, could not tend their lands much during the long, cold winters typical of that region. Of course, some people are very busy. This includes schoolteachers and their students, as well as successful shopkeepers. As will be discussed in a moment, I have also met entrepreneurial families who engage in multiple activities in order to maximise their opportunities in a rapidly changing marketplace. Overall, though, I would note the *lack* of intense, time-consuming work as a characteristic of the places where I've lived during fieldwork over the years. The second observation is that much of what people do by way of work in these communities requires only relatively low levels of skill – as they see it. Obviously, farming and fishing are skilled activities, and so too running a shop, driving a truck, being a cadre or schoolteacher,

---

[9] With reference to what I have already said in the Preface, a sentence of this kind is bound to raise questions for some readers about the representativeness of my study population. More specifically, in the context of today's China – in which everyone appears to be remarkably busy – it may seem anachronistic to talk about people who are not that busy. But the broader point I make in this section, concerning the focus on social aspects of economy, is one that I believe to be very broadly applicable across China as a whole.

etc. I always find it a bit incredible what people manage to do. But when I've talked with them about their own economic lives, they have tended *not* to inflate the significance of skills as such. They consider much of what is done around them by way of work to be unremarkable and the knowledge required for it to be 'common sense' (*changshi*) and/or 'easily learned' (*haoxue*).

What I'm getting at with these two points is that *work as such* does not seem to be a privileged domain of life for most people I have met. It is thus hard for me to see some essential part of their humanity being 'realised' via the activity of farming, fishing, shopkeeping, etc.[10] However, and this is my third observation, they *do* seem passionate about economic activity. They seem to have a very keen interest in money, wealth, prices, debt, fraud and speculation, among other things. Above all, they put a great deal of mental energy into the social side of economy – in how best to deal with their customers, co-workers, etc., and especially with the close circle of kin and non-kin partners with whom their economic lives are most deeply entangled. This relates to a fourth observation, which is that most of them seem relatively uninterested in consumption *except* to the extent that it is an aspect of sociality. Some people I've met enjoy consuming certain things, e.g. expensive brands of cigarettes. But most of them live rather modestly in terms of housing, dress and consumer goods, while simultaneously investing large sums – relative to their level of wealth – in sociality-oriented activities such as life-cycle rituals, gift giving, banqueting and gambling. In sum, then, I want to suggest that the main focus of their aggregate *attention* as economic agents is human relationships. And whereas I find it hard to think of production or consumption per se as the ultimate source of self-education

[10] Note that this is not the same as saying that these occupations don't matter in other ways. For example, fishing as an occupation has very significant implications for personal identity; in other words, you really *are* a fisherman, and it heavily shapes how people think of you.

for the particular group of people that I've studied, I do not find it as hard to think of economic agency more broadly defined – and in particular seen as a general *social* activity, as playing this role.

* * *

During my time in rural northeast China, I met a charming and energetic middle-aged couple, Mr and Mrs Song.[11] They had a close and warm relationship and clearly thought of themselves as a team. Most mornings, they got up and walked to the top of the hill behind the small town of Western Cliff, where they lived, in order to exercise but also to contemplate things and talk. According to their friends, there was something a little man-like about her personality and woman-like about his – a good combination, I was told. They had a son, an only child who had recently moved away to attend a private university in the nearest city. Over the years, they had worked at various jobs, and as the post-Mao reform era progressed, they had become part-time entrepreneurs. He was still a rural cadre (with a bureaucratic rather than an explicitly political job), and in the fairly recent past she had been a schoolteacher. But they also set up several businesses along the way: a restaurant, a small hotel, and a sand-dredging operation along a creek.

The most striking thing about this couple, for me, was their intense focus on cultivating friendships and 'connections' (*guanxi*). This is not unusual in post-Mao China; indeed, anthropologists have documented it extensively (among many others, see Yang 1994). But the Songs were more relentless about this focus than most people I've met. They told me they went into the restaurant trade because they were inviting people for meals so often that they felt it would be 'more convenient' simply to have their own place. I found Mr Song to be a kind of genius at handling the etiquette of banquets, formal or informal. On meal-sharing occasions – be it

---

[11]   During this period of fieldwork I was accompanied for some weeks by Mr Hu Zeheng, who acted as my research assistant. Some of the material in the paragraphs below comes from life history interviews that were carried out by him, and I am very grateful for his help.

with colleagues, important guests, local gangsters – he could be counted on to say some funny and interesting things and to make the kinds of genuinely moving speeches that help cement ties between people.

In the context of all of my fieldwork experiences, then, the Songs present both a typical and atypical case. As per my comments earlier, they seem much busier than average. But they do not seem passionate about work per se. In our conversations, they did not express a strong interest in the details of their jobs, and both had quit or taken periods of leave from employment they'd held over the years. It did not seem that being a cadre, a schoolteacher, a restaurateur, etc., was much of a vocation for them. What they seemed to care about passionately was entrepreneurial activity in general and the excitement of collaboratively making things happen. In spite of having had some success, they lived modestly and, like most of my acquaintances, seemed relatively uninterested in consumption. In a life-history interview, Mrs Song said, 'I have pretty low requirements when it comes to material things. If I had wanted things I wouldn't have married Mr Song! Back then, I had wealthy suitors who told me they could buy whatever I wanted. But I only cared about the quality of the person.' Still, relative to their wealth, they do spend significant sums on banqueting, gift exchange and so on – that is, on sociality-linked, network-enhancing consumption.

* * *

And yet an important point needs to be added here. If one only attended the meals that the Songs share with friends, family and colleagues, at which warm things are said, their relationships would come across in idealised form. In discussing life away from the banquet table, however, they spoke openly about the bitterness entailed in actually having to do things with others. For instance, their hotel venture, started with non-kin partners – another married couple – came to an abrupt end. The problem, they said, was that these partners lacked the will and the ability to truly help with the business, which was labour intensive, and this became a serious source of friction. Mrs Song's preference was to buy them out and keep the hotel so they could run it profitably alone. But in the end, in line with Mr Song's preference, they took the financially disadvantageous step of selling so as to protect their own reputations. He did not want it publicly said that they had fallen out with, and might have taken advantage of, their partners, so they 'amicably' sold the business and looked for other opportunities.

In an interview in which she discussed this experience, Mrs Song also spoke of her parents' experiences of having their life ambitions thwarted by the hell, if you like, of other people. At one point, her father became involved in timber wholesaling. He was just starting out but had done well. As a result, he quit his salaried job and put everything into timber, hoping to earn enough to cover his sons' marriage costs. But then a terrible thing happened: his entire stock was impounded – by corrupt officials, Mrs Song claimed – and sold through the 'back door' for someone else's profit. Everything was lost. Her mother, too, had faced grave disappointment, albeit much earlier in life. A capable student, she was well educated for a rural girl of her time. This gave her opportunities to work as a teacher or administrator. However, her family was dominated by a tradition-minded uncle who found it shameful for women to work outside the home. When she was offered a job, he refused permission for her to accept it, even after she drank pesticide as a protest. As Mrs Song's mother saw things, her whole life trajectory, and subsequently her family's, had been disastrously held back.

Note that these stories, even in outline form, illustrate three types of problems that can occur (and undoubtedly do frequently occur) when interacting with others in the flow of economic life:

1. Problems involving *one's own kin*, e.g. the uncle who blocks the career of Mrs Song's mother
2. Problems involving *familiar non-kin counterparts*, e.g. the couple with whom the Songs set up the failed hotel venture

3. Problems involving *unfamiliar non-kin counterparts*, who in some cases are strangers, e.g. the cadres who expropriated the timber business of Mrs Song's father

The details changed a lot, of course, and yet such stories emerged spontaneously whenever people I came to know were asked (in the context of semi-structured life-history interviews) to say something about how things had gone thus far in life, with a particular steer to focus on economy. To a great extent, it seems, their experience of economic agency *is* the experience of dealing with problems of these kinds as they come up – alongside happier, at times actually exhilarating, experiences of doing things together with others and it working out.

* * *

At the start of this chapter, I suggested that the most important thing we learn about as economic agents is ourselves; more specifically, we come to learn about the cooperative species essence that all humans share. A crucial aspect of this, I suggest, is the ongoing struggle that we have with the intrinsically difficult ethics of cooperation. But the formulations I am using here rest on a number of terms – economic agency, ethics, cooperation, self-education, species essence – the meanings of which are far from obvious. So, at this point let me say a bit more precisely what it is that I have in mind.

As should be obvious by now, when I refer in this book to *economic agency* I mean not only working for a wage, buying goods in markets, etc., i.e. activities that we might think of as prototypically 'economic'. As an anthropological substantivist, I have in mind as well the much broader set of activities through which humans transform the world, themselves and each other, while securing a livelihood in history. Note that while Marx has sometimes been criticised by anthropologists for having an overly 'economistic' view of human nature – i.e. a view that is too narrowly focused on economic activity narrowly defined – I believe that my own broad definition is consistent with what he (and Hegel before him) had in mind when theorising about economic agency and about human self-education. Crucially, economic agency as understood by substantivists/Marxists extends both to

- activities that in our normal folk understandings might fall under the rubric of 'family and kinship' rather than 'economics' per se, including the intrafamilial activities through which we produce and sustain new generations of labour power within households, and
- activities that in our normal folk understandings might fall under the rubric of 'broader patterns of sociality' rather than 'economics' per se, including the extrafamilial activities through which we produce and sustain social and economic ties within and between communities.

This very broad way of defining economic agency is holistic in two senses. First, it is holistic in implying that more or less 'everything' is *potentially* relevant to economic agency – including kinship, religion and more. Second, it is holistic in assuming that across this decidedly huge domain of 'everything', many analytically significant linkages are there to be found. In a given society, for example, it might be the case that religious rituals play a major role in marriage patterns – and, by extension, in patterns of economic migration. Our economic analysis of that society would thus need to account for ... marriage patterns and rituals. Of course, the goal of economic modelling, as I have already explained at several points in this book, is precisely *not* to have to take 'everything' into account. The *empiricist* approach of anthropology, which is holistic and broadly Marxist in inspiration, could thus be said to stand in stark contrast to the *rationalist* approach of model-building economics, which is atomistic and broadly Utilitarian in inspiration. As I have just been arguing, however, I think we should be careful not to overstate this contrast. In particular, it would be very wrong to claim that Utilitarian approaches, by contrast with anthropological ones, are indifferent to (or unaware of) the moral and ethical implications of our shared economic life, or to the ways in which economic agency is tied to broader patterns of cooperative sociality, e.g. family life and religious conventions. This claim is simply untrue, as even a cursory reading of J. S. Mill and others – including contemporary economists – should make clear.

* * *

Moving on, the term *ethics* as I use it in this book, including in the phrase 'the ethics of cooperation', rests on drawing an ideal-type contrast between morality and ethics. Morality, as I define it here, is about rules and norms (e.g. 'Fathers must always be respected'), whereas ethics is about (a) the attempts we make to live well within complex realities and (b) the conscious evaluations we make of such attempts as they unfold in the course of life (e.g. 'My father is a gambling addict, and I should respect him but I can't quite do so unquestioningly, not to mention that I'm feeling tired today, therefore…'). The helpfulness of making this distinction has been questioned by some.[12] However, I find it helpful in two specific ways (Stafford 2010b), both of which will be elaborated in the passages that follow. First, contrasting ethics with morality helps capture the important truth that ordinary people often – I would suggest as a matter of routine – behave 'ethically' and '*im*morally' at the same time. That is, they break moral rules for reasons that (to them, at least, and under particular circumstances) make some kind of ethical sense. As I will explain in a moment, this has implications for our understandings of human cooperation. Second, the morality/ethics distinction helps clarify some issues that are related to moral *learning*, and that are thus linked to the process of self-education. In brief, it can be argued that once people

---

[12] As Laidlaw (2013) explains, this contrast has been made by many people working within the emerging 'anthropology of ethics', albeit often with different understandings of what the contrast consists in.

acquire moral rules, which are often in fact relatively straightforward and even banal, they do not need to think about them further. Indeed, such rules are typically placed beyond questioning by sociocultural mechanisms. By contrast, a great deal of cognitive attention is focused on ethics, as I define this term. That is, we constantly turn ethical issues over in our minds and debate them publicly, as if there were always something new to be learned from thinking and arguing about them. Finally, note that whereas moral rules clearly vary between cultures, it isn't so obvious that the lived experience of ethics does so to such a great extent. That is, notwithstanding cultural-historical variation in moral rules, we keep coming back, as humans, to the same ethical and existential dilemmas.

* * *

Which brings us to *cooperation*. Cooperation, by any definition one can think of (and in the interdisciplinary literatures there are many[13]), is a pervasive feature of human life. How could it be otherwise? Collective life as we know it could not be sustained without cooperative activity of different kinds. Certainly, anthropologists have long described the forms that cooperation takes in human societies, e.g. how cooperative agricultural labour is organised, how common pool resources are managed, how large-scale ritual activities are put together and so on. However, they have primarily *theorised* cooperation in terms of *reciprocity*, to some extent leaving other types of cooperation aside for analytical purposes. This is partly on the empiricist grounds that in the real-world communities that anthropologists study via fieldwork, systems of reciprocity have such an obvious and unmissable salience (e.g. see Yan's 1993 account of rural north China, where the reciprocal 'flow of gifts' heavily structures social relationships of many different kinds).

Indeed, it is largely as an extension of their interest in reciprocity that anthropologists have come to see the economy as a whole as an

---

[13] For a very useful discussion, one that places the term *cooperation* in the context of debates in evolutionary theory, see West et al. (2007).

intrinsically moral/ethical domain, contrasting themselves with econo-mists who – from a starting point in the study of market transactions under presumed conditions of scarcity – see economy as a domain of self-ishness, and more specifically of utility maximisation by self-interested agents. As I have been suggesting, however, this contrast between anthro-pologists and economists is based at least in part on a caricature of the latter. Both economists and economic psychologists know perfectly well that economic life is a social and collaborative activity rather than an individual and 'atomistic' one. They know that economic life presents human agents with a wide range of ethical dilemmas. The classical economists/Utilitarians certainly understood things in this way, and hoped that our shared economic life could, in some imaginable future, produce consequences that would be beneficial (and thus morally good) for society as a whole. Moreover, the recent research in economic psy-chology, cited earlier, is precisely meant to explore the moral and ethical dispositions that individuals bring to exchange. It is just not the case that scholars engaged in such work are great fans of selfishness, or presume that humans are indifferent to each other – on the contrary.

A key distinction with anthropology, however, is that most such research in economic psychology has focused not on reciprocity between known individuals over the long term – the kind of thing anthropologists study at an intimate level – but rather on one-shot transactions between strangers.[14] The surprising finding, to repeat, is that most people are 'cooperative' even when dealing with strangers. We are inclined to be fair to and shoulder (sometimes significant) costs to the benefit of others with whom we do *not* have sustained ties and who we may never meet again. This evidence, along with other evidence I will discuss further on, has even been used to argue that we are a naturally cooperative species.

[14] This isn't because economists and psychologists think that long-term relationships don't exist or are unimportant. It's because they think (and this is explicitly so for those coming from an evolutionary perspective) that there is something fundamen-tally important about how we deal with strangers.

Nobody would want to suggest, however, that humans find coopera-tion easy. There is plenty of evidence around us that, on the contrary, cooperation is hard and that it is only *thanks* to a range of special mech-anisms that we manage to pull it off. For example, partner selection is a key feature of many types of cooperation, and a point at which coop-eration can and does go wrong (as it did for the Songs in their hotel venture).[15] Perhaps unsurprisingly, then, mechanisms that help us share information about prospective partners – e.g. gossip channels for spreading good/bad reputations – are found across otherwise highly diverse societies. Building on such evidence, Baumard et al. (2013) have developed an evolutionary approach to morality that hinges precisely on these conjoined issues of cooperation, reputation and partner choice. In brief, they argue that humans have a disposition to (genuinely) *want* to be moral in their interactions with others – more specifically, to be 'fair'. This is because those with a disposition of this kind are more likely to be chosen as partners for cooperation, an advantage in evolutionary terms.

Obviously, one can argue against this particular theory, and anthro-pologists will bristle at its evolutionary framing. But I cite it here because it illustrates how an evolved psychological disposition that supports cooperation (the disposition for fairness, something Baumard et al. argue should be found across societies) might have a corollary in a social mechanism – a cultural historical artefact – that supports cooperation (i.e. gossip, something anthropologists would expect to take culturally variable forms, as it clearly does).

* * *

Before moving on to the final two terms, let us return for a moment to the stories shared by the Songs. Are these about *cooperation* per se?

---

[15] This is obviously so when it comes to non-kin cooperation; but note that it may also be true inside kin groups, and especially within large ones (such as Chinese lineages), where agents sometimes have a good deal of flexibility regarding when and with whom to cooperate.

If so, what kinds of *ethical* implications do they entail? For most readers, perhaps only the Songs' failed hotel venture would be seen as a clear case of cooperation gone wrong. Two sides put something into a joint venture, the hotel, with the hope that both would benefit. Moreover, the 'free-riding' problem that emerged in this case is a classic one in our folk understandings of cooperation, whether we call this free riding or not. When their partners were found to be contributing less than their share, the Songs found this hard to take and terminated the business partnership. Notably, however, they did so with careful attention to reputation. Mr Song, in particular, did not think he and his wife should risk being perceived by others as disloyal, as the kind of partners who might cause those with whom they cooperated to 'lose face'. They were prepared to incur costs, i.e. to do something less than maximising their own profit, in order to stop this from happening. (In light of this experience, one thing Mrs Song might have learned is that she and her husband – and perhaps men and women more generally? – have different, and sometimes markedly different, attitudes towards cooperation and reputation.[16])

The case of Mrs Song's mother and her tradition-minded uncle raises a very different set of issues – not least because she did not choose her uncle in the way the Songs chose their business partners. But it too can be interpreted as a cooperation problem of a kind, an intrafamilial one. A young woman and her uncle are caught up in the joint activity of achieving family goals, something to which they both might contribute (e.g. by producing children), and from which they both might benefit (e.g. by receiving elder care). The rules of this family venture are broadly set by the traditional parameters of Chinese kinship and Confucian ideologies, but these leave a great deal of scope for ethical conflict, especially against the background of changing social norms. In my understanding, Mrs Song's mother wanted to work in order to

---

[16] As part of her classic Taiwan-based studies of gender, Margery Wolf discussed the complex gendered politics of gossip and reputation (Wolf 1972).

support her immediate family. Her uncle's primary concern was the public standing of the larger, extended family. He cared more about this collective unit's long-term reputation than about the short-term gain of a single household, and as he saw things, his niece was failing to hold up her side of the (intrafamilial) bargain. She eventually 'cooperated' and did not pursue a career, but this was obviously a coerced outcome. As noted, she drank pesticide, an act of protest meant to draw public attention to her uncle's unreasonable behaviour, thereby harming his/ their reputation. (One thing Mrs Song's mother might have learned is that when cooperation problems within the family go public, one cannot always be sure which relatives will be supportive; indeed, this can be an especially bitter learning experience.)

The case of Mrs Song's father and the corrupt officials may also not strike most readers as a case of cooperation gone wrong. But in the terms of recent interdisciplinary debates, it does make sense to frame it that way. Assuming a generalised culture of corruption, there were resources on the table (the proceeds of the timber business) to be allocated on some basis between Mrs Song's father and the officials – that's how this system works. If the officials were totally self-interested, i.e. 'uncooperative', they would take everything and indeed they had the power to do so because they were de facto dictators in this game. However, they might instead 'cooperate' by letting Mrs Song's father keep everything, or (much more likely) they could do something in between, such as taking a reasonable amount by normal standards and then leaving the rest to him. One reason for doing the latter would be their concern that if their corruption was too flagrant, beyond what was considered tolerable, this could harm their own reputations and perhaps even provoke punishment in some form. (One thing that Mrs Song's father might have learned is that, given the opportunity, some officials will indeed take everything.)

In all three stories, then, reputation is a key consideration. Each story also involves individuals – the less-than-ideal hotel partners, the conservative uncle, the corrupt officials – behaving in what seem to be *un*fair ways. I would stress, however, that the different agents in these stories are likely to have held, and may well have disseminated, very different accounts of what transpired – accounts that shift the *ethical* blame as well as the reputational fallout, or at least complicate it in some way. For instance, the Songs' business partners seem unlikely to agree, just like that, that their contribution to the hotel was any less than the Songs' – in which case, who is to blame for its failure? Who behaved badly? What do *they* say about it? As for the timber business, it may seem obvious that the corrupt officials are the villains. However, it is possible, first, that they themselves would give a very different account of what occurred. Perhaps the venture was illegal and was shut down in order to enforce the law, with the story about corruption circulating easily because people in China are dubious about the law ever being enforced in a selfless way. And, second, even if this *is* a straightforward corruption case, the *ethics* of corruption in China are complex. Many officials feel that they have no choice but to engage in some level of corruption because to *not* do so is to opt out of the system as it functions. Of course, they may still be labelled corrupt, and therefore be seen as morally flawed. But they might argue that this is in order to maintain their position in a system that, on the whole, is good, and moreover that their ultimate aim is to provide for dependents – which means they are not acting out of self-interest, narrowly conceived. What is both ethically and practically tricky is to do all of this and stay in the system while managing the reputational (and other) risks involved.

Then there is the tradition-minded uncle who blocked the career path of Mrs Song's mother. Perhaps this one is clear-cut? Certainly, it may seem obvious that right was on her side. She took a huge risk in protesting her uncle's dominance by drinking pesticide (along with actual suicide, this has been a common form of protest for women in patriarchal China). And yet from the traditional point of view, the uncle behaved morally, at least technically so, in defending family honour, whereas her behaviour could be seen as wrong. In my terminology, I would rather say that her 'immoral' behaviour was *ethical*, i.e. she took on traditional values but in the service of goodness under complex and ever-changing circumstances (again, see Stafford 2010b). Moreover, complications of this kind are very typical of ethical life as it is experienced in the real world – including when we have no choice but to cooperate with others and in doing so must deal with the demands of the (evolving) social worlds that surround us. Thus it is that ethical complications permeate our life stories and keep us awake at night, years later.

* * *

Which brings us, finally, to the remaining two terms on my list: *self-education* and *species essence*. As per my comments earlier on, by 'self-education' I mean the process of learning through which humans come both to actualise and, crucially, to *know* their species essence. But what exactly *is* this species essence, and what would enable us to learn about and grasp it while simultaneously actualising it? The philosopher Allen Wood is again a useful guide. As he points out, when Marx writes about species essence (sometimes rendered as 'species being'), it is not always clear what exactly he has in mind. At certain points, he is simply commenting on the general truth that humans are a social and thus intrinsically cooperative species:

The stress [in some passages of Marx] is on the idea that human beings are essentially connected to their species because the human being is by nature a 'herd animal' or 'social animal', an animal who dwells with others of the same kind and survives by living and working in some sort of cooperative relationship with them. (Wood 2004: 18, comment in brackets added)

This is straightforward, perhaps even banal. But there is something else in Marx's comments about our cooperativeness, a point that is explicitly cognitive and thus directly relevant to the issue of self-education:

Marx says that the human being is a species being 'in that he makes his own species his object', and 'behaves toward, is conscious of or relates to … himself as to the present, living species.' In these remarks [by way of contrast with the remarks in the previous quotation, which simply describe the way in which we live and which might be said with regard to any 'herd animal'] the emphasis seems to be on the *consciousness* which men and women have of their interdependence, or of conduct that is consciously oriented to this interdependence. (Wood 2004: 18, comment in brackets added)

For Marx, in short, the species essence of humans is to be cooperative but also – crucially – to grasp this cooperativeness and, moreover, to take it not only as *an* object of reflection and action but actually as *the* object of human self-education, i.e. the means by which we learn the most essential thing about ourselves.

Just to complicate things further, however, here let me add an important point. Marx's account of self-education, in line with that of Hegel and the other German idealists, is explicitly non-individualistic. In other words, of course it is true that an individual might learn this or that via activity in the world, but he does not ultimately treat self-education via economic agency as a 'mind-internal' activity of individual agents. On the contrary, and firmly in line with the philosophical tradition on which he builds, he takes the intrinsically social or distributed nature of human cognition as a given. In the work of Marx's predecessor Ficthe, we find that 'The concept of a rational [human] being … is essentially the concept of a community, not of an individual' (Wood 2014: 220). And in the work of his immediate predecessor, Hegel, we find that the development of self-consciousness in humans is seen 'as necessarily involving a relation to other people, as inherently social' (Pippin 2010: 19). Thus it is for Marx. To properly know oneself as a human being is to be embedded in a cooperative form of life – one in which individual and collective psychology are mutually implicated, i.e. in which our cognition is 'cooperative' too.

I suppose that most anthropologists, having read this, might observe with satisfaction that Marx's anti-individualism is just another reason that his approach to economy is so much more attractive than that of the utility-obsessed economists and of the psychologists, with their thinking 'individuals'. That being so, let me add a brief word about recent studies of cooperation by developmental psychologists – studies that offset this comparison by bringing it up to date. A large number of studies, the most influential of which have come from Michael Tomasello and his colleagues, suggest that human infants and children, by comparison with their close primate relatives, are strongly disposed to behave in ways that contribute to successful cooperation. Again, this does not mean that they find cooperation easy. It means, rather, that they have good skills and dispositions in place for it – more specifically, that they are disposed to help others, to share things with others, to take on roles for the sake of carrying out activities with others, to care a lot about the rules (no matter how arbitrary) that structure joint activity with others, etc. Crucially, they are disposed to read the intentions of the people around them and, by extension, to 'share intentions' with these other people. And this, according to Tomasello, is the most important of our evolved psychological attributes. It is basically *the* thing that supports human cooperation, enabling as it does the coordination of activity in a deep sense. It makes it possible not only for humans to do small everyday things together, such as moving tables and chairs around a room, but also to sustain cultural practices and social institutions over long stretches of historical time (Tomasello 2009). In other words, and further to what I have said before, if our most essential attribute as humans is our cooperativeness, this extends to our thinking too, premised as it is on the sharing of intentions.

Of course, this is an evolutionary argument. The recent findings suggest that humans everywhere *are* disposed to cooperate, to 'be fair', to share intentions, etc. We therefore do not need to *learn* to cooperate, in this sense. And yet, in the flow of life we clearly encounter – and learn much in relation to – a range of cultural-historical artefacts (ideas, values, objects, practices) that scaffold cooperation in actual societies. Moreover, the endless complexity of cooperation, and especially its *ethical* complications, means that we always have something new to trouble ourselves with. And this object of reflection – the intrinsically difficult ethics of cooperation – permeates all the things we might label as economic psychology: decision making, life planning, the acquisition of work skills and so on. It impinges heavily on the input side of Utilitarian economic psychology (are we going to be cooperative or selfish during transactions with others?) as well as the output side (what form of life, built around what forms of cooperation, would make us happy and/or give us wellbeing?), not to mention – as I am suggesting here – that it impinges heavily on self-education in Hegelian/Marxist terms. In sum, the 'self' that we discover via economic agency is (a) an intrinsically cooperative self that (b) finds cooperation a struggle and thus (c) finds it an object of endless ethical reflection and learning. This is our essence.

✳ ✳ ✳

So where does this leave the Utilitarians? Is their approach so different from that found in Marx?[17] I have already noted above that they too have been keenly interested in questions of moral development and, one could say, in the question of human self-education. Adam Smith (whose relationship to Utilitarianism, again, remains a matter of debate) famously wrote two major books and apparently felt that the one about moral sentiments was more important than the one about *The Wealth of Nations*. If the latter presents humans as intrinsically self-interested (although, as Noam Chomsky has observed, this is a very questionable way of characterising Smith's intention[18]), the former – his *Theory of*

---

[17] The philosopher Allen Wood makes some thought-provoking comments on the relationship between Marxism and Utilitarianism, putting Marx's presumed disdain for Utilitarian philosophers in a broader context (Wood 2004: 147–51); he also has interesting things to say about the comparison between Marx and Adam Smith (Wood 2004: xx–xxiii).

[18] See Noam Chomsky's provocative and thought-provoking comments on Adam Smith, as well as his comments about Mill and Humboldt (Chomsky 1996).

Moral Sentiments – presents them as deeply embedded in social ties. To be a proper person, he suggests, is to cultivate a sympathy for what those around us are feeling and thinking, i.e. to live immersed in inter-subjectivity (a point, by the way, that has significant overlap with recent work by psychologists on cooperation, intention sharing and mind reading).

Meanwhile, J. S. Mill's influential book *On Liberty* is explicitly framed with reference to Humboldt's account of human self-education. And Humboldt himself emerged from the same idealist tradition that so heavily influenced Marx. While *On Liberty* is a book about individual-ism written by a Utilitarian, it is *not* a book that elevates individuals above society, nor one that pretends that social constraints do not – or should not – exist. Mill's main concern, in fact, is that human freedom and creativity is always at risk of being seriously impeded, be it by the force of tradition or by oppressive political-economic regimes. This seems a reasonable thing to fear. But he does not argue that we will be free by being alone and blindly pursuing self-interest; on the contrary. Notably, Mill expert Joseph Persky argues that Marx's work shares deep similarities with that of Mill – notwithstanding the former's occasional harsh words about the latter (not to mention his even harsher words about Bentham). Among other things, Persky notes that 'There is very little distance between Mill's emphasis on self-development and Marx's own discussion of "species [essence]"' (2016: 157).

In fact, a version of this same point was made years ago – albeit in a highly critical voice – by the anthropologist Marshall Sahlins in his influential text *Culture and Practical Reason*. Sahlins's general conclu-sion is that Marxist ideas actually map closely onto Utilitarian ones, much to their detriment (Sahlins 1976). In short, he argues that both are based on universalist, economistic and Western theories of human nature. They thus tend to ignore the role played by history and cul-ture, which Sahlins takes to be the defining and distinctive feature of human experience in the world. I suppose that most Marxist-oriented anthropologists would reject Sahlins's charge against Marx – not least in light of the deep interest he shared with Engels in the cultural-historical determinants of human behaviour – but would be happy for the charge to stand against the Utilitarians. As Persky points out, however, it is hard to read Mill as a universalist, given his commitment to a science of ethology that might help explain cultural-historical variation as a key feature of the human experience.

* * *

Having invoked Marshall Sahlins in passing, I am now obliged to make an anthropological confession as I near the end of this chapter. The stories I have told about the Songs have actually been quite thin by normal ethnographic standards. One obvious thing that is largely missing from my account is the wide range of cultural-historical artefacts that must, by definition, have scaffolded the real-world economic agency of the Songs and those with whom they cooperate. To start with an obvious question in light of my focus on self-education, what, after all, is the Chinese notion of the 'self'? Would not something like an ethically particularistic 'Chinese self' – as theorised by Fei Xiaotong and other China scholars over the years[19] – be a better starting point for any discussion of the Songs and their self-education in history? In truth, most anthropologists would prefer for questions of these kinds to have been raised at the very start of a chapter such as this one rather than near the end, as I am doing here, i.e. on the grounds that this would help us avoid crude universalism when talking about the Songs.

And yet it is equally important, I want to suggest, to bear two key facts about the Songs in mind – facts that would help save us from crude relativism. The first fact, which was the basis of my discussion above concerning the psychology of cooperation, is that the Songs are in the

---

[19] See Fei (1992); note that the introduction to this edition of Fei's book, written by Gary Hamilton and Wang Zheng, contains a useful overview of ideas and theories concerning Chinese selfhood.

same human species as the rest of us. It is hard to see how *any* history can erase this fact, even if it is true that *every* history will heavily shape its consequences. The second fact, which is the basis for the section that follows, is that the Songs are in the same broad flow of (human) history as the rest of us. I want to illustrate this by providing a very brief snapshot of some of the historically particular ways of being that have helped make the Songs what they are today – the point being, to anticipate, that even the most prototypically 'Chinese' aspects of their story cannot be disconnected from our shared human history, which now includes a shared history with respect to both communism and capitalism.[20]

* * *

In many respects, the Songs look like typical products of China's post-Mao era of economic reforms. As a cadre-led family that 'jumped into the sea' of doing business, once this became possible, they fit well into the contemporary moment, one in which a *new* kind of self is widely considered to be emerging in China. This differs from the traditional self, as described by Fei and others, and it has been the subject of considerable scholarship in recent years (e.g. Liu 2002, Yan 2013). It has also been the subject of much debate among ordinary people in China, many of whom understand this new way of being – ambitious, acquisitive, network-extending, etc. – as part and parcel of the nation's opening up. This opening up, in turn, is widely understood by many people as one in which the gaps (including cultural and ideological gaps) between China and the West have narrowed as Maoist collectivism recedes from view.

So, against the background of this recent history, could we say that the Songs have become Westernised – even 'become Utilitarian' – to

[20] Depending on who you listen to, the modern political economy of China is a uniquely Chinese way of delivering Western socialism or a uniquely Chinese way of delivering Western capitalism, or both. The official line is that through market reforms in the post-Mao era, China is delivering 'socialism with Chinese characteristics'; but Yasheng Huang and other observers argue that what has been delivered is capitalism adapted to Chinese political necessities (Huang 2008).

some extent? Actually, a well-known complaint about Utilitarianism/ Consequentialism is that most ordinary people do *not* actually reason or act in what could be called a Utilitarian manner. Among other things, critics point out that the 'trolley problems' invoked by philosophers – specifically, as a way of thinking through the ethical consequences of given actions, such as needing to push somebody off a cliff if we want to save the life of some other person – are highly misleading. They involve situations that are never normally encountered in the real world and imply modes of reasoning that are far from how most ordinary people think. And yet it might be noted, first, that the people I have met during fieldwork in Taiwan and China (including the Songs) certainly do, on the whole, seem very pragmatic in their everyday logic. They are strongly oriented towards consequences such as what will actually make money, thus bringing happiness to their loved ones, and they often explicitly think and talk along those lines. Significantly, this is so even when it implies being flexible towards 'morality', e.g. towards kinship rules that have been imposed a priori by the ancestors, as it were, but that in actual circumstances they might need to 'ethically' deviate from in order to avoid the bad consequences these rules could lead to. (For a fascinating illustration of precisely this process, see James Watson's [1975] article about people who have pragmatic reasons for strongly contravening lineage morality by adopting outsider sons rather than just adopting the sons of their own kinsmen.) All of this implies some version of folk Utilitarianism in Chinese ethical reasoning, or so I would like to suggest.

But there is another point to be made in terms of classic Utilitarianism. The default assumption of many people I have met during fieldwork is that those around them will (pragmatically) follow their own interests and do whatever it takes to improve outcomes for themselves, their loved ones and their associates. For example, it is disappointing but not surprising if a cadre takes wealth from others for his own family, as reportedly happened with the timber business of Mrs Song's father.

Corruption of this kind is labelled immoral, but everyone recognises that 'in actual circumstances' it is based on a natural and to some extent *ethical* impulse: to do what benefits one's family (Stafford 2006; see also Yan 2016). Moreover, it is felt that this type of selfishness, so long as it does not get out of hand, actually can lead to good, or at least tolerable, social consequences. Every individual will be taken care of, have well-being, so long as everyone is part of a (selfish and yet ethically motivated and constrained) group.

Importantly, reasoning of this kind, which I do not mean to suggest is just accepted by everyone, is intrinsic to popular Chinese views of the world rather than being a Western import specific to life in a modern market economy. More generally, 'Utilitarian' ways of living that are sometimes spoken of as new to China's post-Mao era may not, in fact, be new at all. As explained, it is widely held in China that the post-Mao self is more oriented to personal gain than the traditional one. However, as Hill Gates has shown, China actually has a very old tradition of petty capitalism – one going back to the Song dynasty – in which gain of some kinds has been seen as morally acceptable and even admirable (Gates 1996). The point, then, is not only that China is (and has been) sharing a history with us, e.g. that Western ideas have circulated in China for some time. It is also true that Chinese people have behaved in ways we might *think* of as characteristically modern or Western or Utilitarian but that in fact are very old – certainly predating the birth of the Utilitarian philosophers, not to mention predating the birth of modern capitalism.

Meanwhile, note that the Songs, however Utilitarian in outlook they could be said to be now, are also Maoists – and thus Marxists of a kind. Mr Song is a life-long party member, a cadre, and someone who seems genuinely committed to Maoism as an ethical practice centred on cooperative social life as a political end. At least some of the values embedded in this way of being were acquired by him via explicit pedagogy. This happened during his early years in the countryside, but also more recently in his role as a cadre – something that involves attending a succession of workshops and study groups, not to mention drinking sessions and banquets during which party policy is discussed. Of course, the relationship of Maoism to Marxism – and beyond that to Marx's roots in German/European idealist philosophy – is an incredibly complex topic. But it's not as if the historical connections from Europe to China aren't very substantive. Meanwhile, I would add that many of the people I have met during fieldwork who, unlike Mr Song, have little connection to politics proper (be they from mainland China with its complex legacy of Maoism or from Taiwan with its complex legacy of anti-Maoism) could equally be called folk Marxists. They are more 'collectivist' than 'individualist' in world view and do not, in my experience, appear to believe that fulfilment will come via wealth or material consumption per se. Many of them (like good Marxists) see the process of economic agency itself as potentially elevating, even spiritually improving, because it entails doing things with and for others – however disillusioning this may be in practice.

And then, as I learned, the Songs are Confucians too. They spontaneously express traditional-sounding opinions about family and kinship, from time to time, in spite of their commitment to a Maoism which has often been explicitly anti-family in practice. For example, they have provided long-term care and support to his elderly parents and subsequently to hers, something that has not always been easy. And when it comes to their (only) son, they hold some classic expectations of him, including that *his* selfhood should be tied up with an ongoing process of Confucian-style self-cultivation. So far as I know, Confucian philosophy, as such, has never been a direct object of study for the Songs. Their thoughts and actions as 'Confucian selves' are thus largely based on some of the rather shallow moral truisms widely distributed in China today but also on the – far from shallow – folk ethics transmitted between ordinary people, i.e. an ethics focused on the actual dilemmas of ordinary social life. I might add, by the way, that the anti-familism of

Chinese reformers and revolutionaries, including Mao, came from their deep engagement with the problem of how China could keep up with the West commercially, militarily and scientifically, and at least some of them thought China's familism was the prime sticking point. All of this means that even the stereotypically Chinese attribute of 'being Confucian in outlook' cannot be neatly detached, any more, from the shared flow of human history.

Finally, and perhaps more surprisingly, Mr Song is a Daoist. As I learned from the outset, he is actually the keen follower of a master who gives him advice about money, business, personal ties, health, etc., and who has inserted him into a network of devotees. In my understanding, Daoism provides Mr Song a way to reflect on, cope with and manoeuvre with respect to the apparently random (and often very comical) contingencies of life and of relationships with others, including partners in money making. But what exactly is the Daoist notion of the self and of the process of learning and self-education for humans? There are numerous commentaries on this question, but one widely held formulation has it that Daoism is precisely about the *end* of selfhood and about the realisation of selflessness, which sounds a wonderfully seductive idea, and yet …

* * *

Obviously, much more could be said about each of these orientations that are bundled together in the persons of the Songs. There is a 'new' market-oriented mentality of some kind that might be called Utilitarian – but that, in any case, has antecedents in a Chinese folk pragmatism. There is a Maoism/Marxism (of some kind), a Confucianism (of some kind) and a Daoism (of some kind). Each entails a different understanding not only of the self but also of learning, of cooperation and of the ultimate aims of life. Each is the product of a complex, non-linear history that is partly Chinese but also, equally, part of a shared global/human history (again, this is as true of Confucianism as it is of the market economy). Importantly, in each orientation there is a theory about how one ought to live, a moral theory, but then as well a real-world *ethical* version that is messy and difficult and sometimes troubling. For example, whatever philosophical Daoism may propose in terms of the 'realisation of selflessness', the people I know, certainly including the Songs, use Daoist practice as part of a broader attempt to sort out real-world problems such as how to get along with (difficult) others and/or how to sort out the (difficult) family finances.[21]

Thus it is that my brief outline of some of the cultural-historical artefacts that have scaffolded self-education for the Songs leads me to three general points. The first is the remarkable fact of human diversity: we go in endless directions with our ideas about the self, the world and the ways in which we ought to live in it. The second, which links directly back to Marx's notion that self-education is actually *impeded* by capitalism, is that it is hard to specify what kind of system the Songs are now living in. It is some kind of diverse/hybrid system in which the ongoing self-education of individuals (or possible failures in this) cannot easily be pinned down to 'communism', 'capitalism' or anything else (I will discuss this further in Chapter 6).[22] And then the third point, which follows from

[21] Note that although Daoism in theory is (or may be) about the realisation of selflessness, the actual practice of Daoism is very much about actual human relationships – be they between masters and apprentices or between people who live in communities together and who engage in collective acts of worship. In saying this, I am not at all denying the significance of philosophical Daoism and its view of the world, simply noting that transcending cooperation is one thing to achieve in theory and another thing to achieve in practice. As the case of Mr Song shows, even somebody who 'is' Daoist may be many other things as well – including a striving entrepreneur who is super keen to make useful connections!

[22] To borrow James Carrier's (1992) terminology, I would say that the Songs live in a semi-traditional world that is not that far along the path of 'emerging alienation' that comes with full-blown capitalism. This makes it rather trickier to say to what extent the (hybrid) system in which they live should, in Marxist terms, impede the process of self-education. My argument here, in any case, is that the process of self-education: we cannot liberate ourselves from the species essence we 'discover' via experience in the world.

the previous one, is the fact that none of these orientations – including the Daoist one that would, ideally, just do away with the self altogether – manages to escape the fundamental problems that we humans as a species essence face.

One might thus conclude that there is both good news and bad news for my ideal type of Marxism in the story of self-education that I have told in this chapter. The good news is that we are indeed a cooperative species – much more so than was appreciated at the historical moment when Marx himself was writing. Indeed, it seems to me that he would find the recent scientific work on cooperation (and perhaps especially the work of developmental psychologists on cooperation, which I think everyone interested in human behaviour and society ought to read) a remarkable achievement, deeply relevant to his own concerns in the nineteenth century with how cooperativeness makes humans what they are and with how this plays itself out in history. The fact that some of the recent work proceeds from what could be called a Utilitarian starting point that does not on the surface seem very Marxist would, I think, not have worried him greatly. Not only *are* we cooperative, we also have *consciousness* of this fact – i.e. we take our essential cooperative-ness, as filtered by its ethical consequences, as our object of thought. Having said this – and here is the bad news – while our entanglement in cooperative life might generate forms of self-education, in the Marxist/Hegelian sense, it is also true that the difficulties of cooperation and of sociality more generally are truly absorbing for humans. Indeed, these difficulties seem just as absorbing and intractably 'enchanting' for us as any form of ideology. One can thus argue – contra Marx – that absorption and enchantment of this kind is bound to persist regardless of the political-economic system in which we live, and that we can never manage to transcend and/or learn our way out of it.

SIX

The Politics of Cognition

The subject matter of social anthropology is sometimes broken down into the four very general domains of 'politics', 'economics', 'kinship' and 'religion'. This categorisation is adopted, at least in part, simply as a matter of convenience. However, it does have a certain logic to it and has some practical implications as well. For example, the publication track record of an economic anthropologist will normally look very different from that of an anthropologist of kinship. And while the syllabus for a course in economic anthropology is likely to cover such topics as markets, labour relations and debt, the syllabus for a course in anthropology of kinship is likely to cover such topics as birth, adoption, marriage and bridewealth.

In our everyday teaching practice, however, we are quick to deconstruct this schema, telling even first-year students in introductory courses that it doesn't hold up that well in reality. Indeed, this is one of the basic lessons of anthropology, which is premised on an especially strong version of human science holism. To return to bridewealth, one of our anthropology of kinship topics, whatever else such marriage payments may do, they often have massive financial implications for the families that give or receive them. When I was carrying out fieldwork in Dragon Head, in rural north-east China, the cost of marriage was certainly one of the main topics of conversation. The price of 'buying' a bride for one's son had literally gone through the roof, at that moment, and for many families this was thus the most consequential economic event of their lives. (As my fieldwork interlocutors put it, those who happened to have given birth to daughters under China's one-child policy were now suddenly striking it rich.) So, should marriage payments of these kinds be studied under the heading of kinship or economics? Meanwhile, there are many societies in which family ancestors are honoured via rituals for the dead, as evidenced by the elaborate ancestral temples that are dotted around Protected Mountain, in rural south-west China. Not only are the ancestors remembered in these temples, they are actually worshipped, and the distinction between gods, ghosts and family ancestors is not nearly as clear cut in the Chinese belief system as one might imagine it would be. Does the fact of ancestor worship in China (and elsewhere) pertain to religion or to kinship? These worshipped ancestors were our relatives, after all. And then, to give one final example, there are many societies in which aspects of local governance are, or have been, organised along family lines. In pre-revolutionary China, lineages and clans sometimes performed important political functions at the local level, and as part of this activity often took a leading role in the economy. Should this be understood as an aspect of kinship, politics or economics? Presumably, the correct answer is that it falls (or at least could be said to fall) within all three.

When it comes to economics in the contemporary West, everyone knows that it is deeply entangled with politics. To give an obvious illustration, setting interest rates is an explicitly political act. This is true no matter how hard we might try to keep the politics out of it, e.g. by establishing independent central banks and monetary policy committees, as has been done in the United Kingdom and other countries. And yet, one of the great divides in the discipline of economics has, of course, been between those who embrace the political entanglements – claiming political economy as the object of study – and those who (while understanding perfectly well that economic life is totally political) attempt to separate things out, to the extent that this is possible. They do so in the hope of defining a tractable object for rigorous economic analysis. By contrast, anthropologists, being professional holists, are content to assume that life is always quite complicated and that the boundaries of life are always quite permeable. As an aspect of this permeability, they know that economics is inevitably going to be political – no matter the fieldsite – and moreover that kinship and religion are inevitably going to be political (and economic) too.

Of course, if an anthropologist were asked to specify a representative economic agent from her own fieldsite, she would likely conjure up someone engaged in a prototypical economic activity, e.g. working in a factory, buying and selling goods at a market or running a small business. Many of the people I have met during fieldwork are caught up in everyday activities of these kinds: Mr Su and Mr Li are fisherman, the Sus sell their teas and ices from a market stand, the Songs are small-time entrepreneurs, etc. As I have been suggesting, however, these people also have families and make ceaseless efforts, in the flow of life, to generate and sustain wider networks of sociality – at least in part because they explicitly view this as an *economic* imperative. They also put a lot of energy into worshipping gods and/or ancestors, at least in part because such spirits, in their understanding, have the power to bring *economic* prosperity to the living (or, if not that, at least to protect them from serious impoverishment). For my fieldwork interlocutors, in other words, acts of kinship and religion fall just as much within the domain of economics as anything else. Certainly, such acts are an integral part of making a living and of having a productive and generative life as a social being, in their folk model.

* * *

Bringing kinship, religion, politics and economics together in the classically holistic manner of social anthropologists has a number of analytical consequences, two of which I would like to foreground here (as will be seen, they are interlinked). The first has to do with *gender*. In the case of traditional China, at least, women's contributions to politics and economics were often erased in one form or another. Politics in the public sphere was presumed to be a male domain, as a matter of definition. (The rule of China's only female emperor, Wu Zetian, was taken by Confucian historians as an object lesson in why the emperor should never be a woman.) Meanwhile, women's contributions to economics – however centrally important in reality have also often been marginalised in China, a process deeply tied up with broader patterns of sociocultural transformation (for a fascinating account of this, see Bray's [1997] study of technology and gender across eight centuries). But what about kinship and religion? In fact, it can be argued that Chinese women's contributions to these two domains have *also* been marginalised at many historical moments, i.e. as a consequence of the hegemony of patriarchal ideas across all areas of society and culture. In the classic Confucian understanding, it was the continuation of a male line of descent that really mattered when it came to kinship, and the overwhelming preference was to have sons and grandsons who would be able to continue to worship the (male) ancestors into the foreseeable future. And yet, in the contemporary folk understanding in China and Taiwan, at least as I have observed this via fieldwork, it is explicitly acknowledged that women make crucial contributions to kinship and religion. Moreover, they are felt to exercise a degree of power and influence and autonomy within these particular domains – and probably more so than they do in the more 'public' domains of economics and, especially, politics. Indeed, seen from this perspective, one can even speak of China as being a matriarchal society, at least in a restricted sense.[1] Building on all of this, my first point is actually a relatively simple, but I think important, one. If kinship and religion are separated out from our analyses of economics and politics in China and Taiwan, then women (and women's spheres of influence) can easily start to vanish from view. As a result, our understanding of economics and/or of political-economy could be impoverished.

---

[1] Stafford (2000, 2008a).

This, in turn, relates to my second point. If kinship and religion are separated out from our analysis of economics and politics in China and Taiwan, then our understanding of *self-education* as the end of economic life could also be impoverished. It is one thing to say that we learn from working together in the course of productive activities such as waged labour, or while exchanging things with others, e.g. when we hand over money for goods at the market. It is another thing to say that we learn from social activities that are 'non-economic' by standard definitions but that are nevertheless integral to the production and reproduction of human life and sociality as we know it, including activities in the domains of kinship and religion as these are typically understood – not least the production and nurturance of children and their protection via religious rituals and other practices.

If economic agency is defined as being primarily, or wholly, about material production and exchange, and about the political infrastructure that relates directly to this, then what we *might* be said to learn from economic agency, in many cultural-historical environments, is that we are part of a fundamentally competitive species (with a 'surprisingly' cooperative streak) – one in which the default economic agent is male, it seems. If, by contrast, economic agency is defined as having as much or more to do with the production and reproduction of life and of sociality, then what we *might* be said to learn from economic agency, in many cultural-historical environments, is that we are part of a fundamentally cooperative species (with a 'surprisingly' competitive streak) – one in which the default economic agent is female, or at least as likely to be female as male. To put this differently, our way of defining economy and economic agency is bound to profoundly shape our understanding of what it means, or could mean, for humans to be caught up in the process of self-education – and also where this process might eventually lead to.

But here let me return to the studies of human cooperation that I introduced in Chapter 5. In fact, there is considerable variation across this diverse interdisciplinary field when it comes to the types of 'cooperation' that scholars examine empirically and thus also theorise from. Should our focus be on the extent to which individual agents cooperate with each other (or not) during market-type transactions between strangers? Or, given the evolutionary history of our species, should the prototypical site of human cooperation be seen in the hunting (or perhaps gathering) activities that our ancestors engaged in, and whatever the modern equivalents of these might be? Obviously, cooperating with complete strangers during a market transaction and cooperating with known others during a hunting/gathering party are two radically different kinds of human activity. One thing they both share, however, is that most of us would, I think, easily classify both of them (i.e. both market exchange and hunting/gathering) as intrinsically 'economic'. Now, what about cooperation in the provision of childcare? The argument of the evolutionary anthropologist Sarah Hrdy is that if we are looking for the origins of the exceptional cooperativeness to be found in the human species – to go back to the Marxist terminology, if we are looking for the origins of our *species essence* – we should look not at hunting parties, for example, but rather at cooperation in the provision of childcare (Hrdy 2011).[2] Hrdy's account of the role played by alloparenting (in effect, distributed childcare) in human evolution further supports the argument that when considering economic agency as the site for human self-education, we should define it in what anthropologists would consider a *non*-economistic way. In other words, kinship and broader patterns of sociality should be fully part of the mix, which in turn will give us a totally different idea of what learning-while-cooperating looks like. As an aspect of this, I would want to argue that religion (by the broad definition I am using) should be part of the mix as well, i.e. on the grounds of its foundational role in the creation of the social on which economic life in human communities is ultimately premised. And then, perhaps, women's roles in economic life will also be reconceived.

***

2 For a succinct overview of Hrdy's theory, see Konnor (2011).

As I will discuss in a moment, the question of how kinship and religion should be understood in relation to politics and economics –
including in relation to cooperative economic agency – has special
relevance when it comes to comparing self-education in China and
Taiwan. This is partly because these two places have had very different modern histories with respect to Chinese 'tradition'. Before turning to that topic, however, I would like to insert a brief discussion
here of the politics of cognitive science in general and of the politics
of cognitive anthropology in particular. As will be seen, this is also
directly relevant to the question of human self-education that I will
take up further on.

Near the start of her detailed account of the history of cognitive science, Margaret Boden makes some comments about the 'science wars'
debates that were taking place in the mid to late twentieth century, in
the era when cognitive science in its modern form was also emerging on
the scene (Boden 2006: 21–37). In line with the anti-establishment tenor
of the time, the credibility of science in general came under question,
in part on the constructivist grounds that 'facts' must be understood
as social/historical/political phenomena rather than something that is
simply out there in the world waiting to be discovered (e.g. by scientists).
Beyond this very general questioning of science as a practice, however,
some of the issues up for debate in this era were directly pertinent to the
emergence of cognitive science and its reception. These included, among
other things, concerns about the use to which computers and other new
information technologies might be put (including misgivings about computer processes being used as a model for 'how humans think'); concerns
about government and corporate funding of the science-technology
nexus (including the worry that such funding would crowd out critical social science and humanities perspectives); and concerns about the
application of cybernetics, game theory and related approaches to the
understanding of – and also possible 'engineering' of – a wide range of
social phenomena.

Being a generally radical discipline, anthropology was perhaps quite open to the idea that science as a practice should come under critical scrutiny. And although anthropology is an *empiricist* discipline, it also happens to be quite open to constructivism in various forms. After all, the basic cultural relativist premise to be found at the heart of empiricist anthropology is a classic form of constructivism. Beyond this, as I have explained, anthropologists have always been averse to universalistic psychology, and in particular they have condemned the premises of *evolutionary* psychology. These, they have argued, all too easily lead us to a crude type of determinism in which every human behaviour, no matter how complex, is said to have some evolutionary 'cause'. In *Anthropology and the Cognitive Challenge*, Maurice Bloch has discussed the background to all of this in detail – including the concern that cognitive and evolutionary approaches might legitimate racist/racialist/sociobiological theorising of the kind that anthropologists abhor (Bloch 2012).

But here I want to frame the issue in a somewhat different way, putting aside the *potentially* objectionable politics of cognitive anthropology in order to ask, what are the *actual* politics of cognitive anthropology? Let me explain what I intend by this. It might be argued that cognitive anthropology, by focusing on 'mind-internal' phenomena (if that is what cognitive anthropologists can be said to do), errs in ignoring the political-economic grounding of human mental life. This is a sin of omission, so far as most anthropologists are concerned. And if one reads, just to give one example, Norbert Ross's useful overview of the field, *Culture and Cognition*, it is indeed the case that politics is largely absent from his account. The index to Ross's book doesn't include such topics as power, politics, hierarchy or inequality (Ross 2004). It might also be argued that cognitive anthropology has erred in actually siding with a scientific or positivist agenda (if that is what cognitive anthropologists do) as opposed to a critical human science agenda – a sin of association. But, again, what about the explicit politics of cognitive anthropology as it is practised?

Here I will not provide a detailed overview; I am simply pulling out a few indicative cases from the (quite heterogeneous) subfield of psychology-oriented anthropology. Certainly, some proportion of the research within this subfield is explicitly political. More importantly for me, by a generous interpretation one could argue that *all* of it is at least implicitly political, bearing as it does on the core issue of how humans come to know, understand and act on the world. But what this means can obviously vary a lot.

Take the case of Jean Lave. Among many other things, she has studied the use of mathematics in everyday life activities such as grocery shopping. Her writing on this topic does not, on the surface, appear to be very political at all. In reality, however, Lave's whole approach is framed in relation to an explicitly 'historicised' model of learning within communities of practice, one based in a Marxist/materialist understanding of human cognition, activity and real-world practice (Lave 1988). A different kind of example is found in the recent work of the psychological anthropologists Naomi Quinn and Jeanette Marie Mageo on psychological attachment theory (Quinn & Mageo 2013). This theory is based on evolutionary premises, and Quinn and Mageo thus articulate the standard anthropological critique of such approaches, i.e. that they fail to take account of cultural-historical variation. Beyond this, however, some of the criticisms they make of attachment theory (and they are not the first to do so) are explicitly political ones. Not only is attachment theory ethnocentric, it is also normative: it has become the hegemonic model by which good parenting and child development is measured in much of the world, with implications in particular for women.

Or consider the case of Arthur Wolf. By contrast with Lave, but also by contrast with Quinn and Mageo, Wolf takes what is very much a science-oriented approach to the study of human psychology. He engages with evolutionary premises of the kind that most (critical) social and cultural anthropologists firmly reject. More specifically, building on Edward Westermarck's work on how our 'moral emotions' relate to cultural variation in moral systems, Wolf has studied the evolution of incest aversion in our species. He looks in particular at the few empirical cases where Westermarck's theory of incest aversion can be put to a direct test, centrally including the case of Chinese 'little daughter-in-law' marriage that I briefly mentioned in Chapter 4. Wolf's argument, in short, is that we *do* have an evolved aversion to close-kin incest – as Westermarck predicted – notwithstanding the significant cultural variation to be found around the world when it comes to actual marriage practices and actual incest taboos. Indeed, Wolf tells a fascinating story about the extent to which the cultural-historical artefacts surrounding marriage and incest have been shaped and constrained by the existence of this important evolved aversion. Further to this, the whole point of his final book on the subject was to show how the incest aversion has been exploited in historically variable ways, specifically as an aspect of *power* in traditional societies (Wolf 2014). As this suggests, Wolf's work is certainly not apolitical, nor is his analysis of the gendered politics of marriage practices in traditional China apolitical, the explicit 'scientism' and evolutionary grounding of his underlying approach notwithstanding. It is hard for me to see how his research could be construed as politically objectionable, i.e. other than the underlying fact that he believes in such a thing as an evolved human nature and he is therefore not anti-science.

Beyond Wolf, there are a number of other psychology-focused anthropologists who have studied topics with clear political ramifications. These include Lawrence Hirschfeld and Rita Astuti, who have studied the development of 'folkbiological' and 'folksociological' knowledge in children, including in relation to questions of identity, ethnicity and race, and Christina Toren, who has studied the development of children's understandings of social hierarchies (Astuti, Solomon & Carey 2004; Hirschfeld 1998; Toren 1990, 1999). The work of Maurice Bloch also provides a clear illustration of the point I am getting at here. His interest in studying human psychology and engaging with academic psychologists emerged directly from his ongoing attempt (framed in a broadly Marxist perspective) to understand the relationship between knowledge and power in human societies. The psychological topics on which he has subsequently focused in his research – including memory, school-based knowledge transmission, deference and the constitution of the self – have virtually always had explicitly political ramifications (Bloch 1998, 2005, 2012, 2013). For Bloch, to repeat the phrase I used in the Preface, there is surely nothing more politically significant than the relationship between human psychology and human history. So far as I know, that is why he has bothered to study psychology, and why he considers it essential for anthropologists to engage with findings and theories from recent cognitive science.

Be that as it may, my experience has been that the use of *any* psychology or cognitive-science orientation leads anthropologists to interpret the research they are hearing about as being apolitical in orientation and potentially dubious. Why? There is something ideological at play in this, I believe, by which I mean that most anthropologists do not even know they are doing this when they do it. So strongly committed are they to the ideology of a non-psychological anthropology that they can't see what is in front of them. They basically interpret politically oriented psychological and cognitive anthropology as an impossibility. And yet, as per the argument in this book, one could say that in pursuing the question of the relation between psychology and history, these anthropologists are doing *exactly* what an intrinsically radical anthropology ought to do. How do we learn to be what we are and to hold the values we hold? As this process of learning, knowing and believing unfolds across time, what is the relationship between our apparently 'individual' (mind-internal) cognition and the distributed – i.e. intrinsically social, and thus always political – cognitive processes in which we are embedded? To what extent are we able to overcome social and/or evolutionary determinants in order to cognise, and actually bring into existence, new ways of being in the world?

* * *

The case of my own work is a bit different. I have never defined myself as a cognitive or psychological anthropologist, and I have never collaborated directly with psychologists. And although I admire work of the kind that, for example, Joseph Henrich and his evolutionary anthropology colleagues have done – that is, on how culturally particular values, beliefs and practices shape responses to experimental economics tasks – I personally have no interest in running ultimatum game experiments (for instance) as part of my own fieldwork practice. Still, as a mainstream social anthropologist, I have always been interested in research and teaching on topics that relate to psychology in some way – e.g. learning, schooling, child development, emotion, identity and so on, not to mention cooperation, the crucially important human science topic that Henrich and his colleagues have studied. Plus I read a lot of psychology.

Based on fieldwork in Taiwan and China, I ended up writing two books – *The Roads of Chinese Childhood* and *Separation and Reunion in Modern China* – that I personally thought of as being not only somewhat psychological in orientation but also political (Stafford 1995, 2000a). The empirical material in the first book focused on learning, schooling, religion and child development. But the whole structure of the book is framed around a juxtaposition between contrasting nationalist and folk views of what children should become, including the – obviously political, I should think – question of whether sons should be prepared to die for the nation *or* should be protected and strengthened (e.g. by ritual means) in order to ensure family continuity. In any case, it has only rarely been cited as having anything to say about politics; it is basically taken as an apolitical book about childhood. My second book focused on rituals and practices of 'separation' and 'reunion' in China and

Taiwan, and on the roles these play in the construction of identities. Again, the political angle is quite explicit, or so it seems to me. Among other things, I focus on the question of the development of historical consciousness, and in one chapter I examine the role that idioms of separation and reunion have played in the highly contentious politics of whether Taiwan should eventually reunite with China. But many of the cases I discuss in the book are, again, to do with children and with the private or domestic sphere of life, which is normally under the control of women. It has almost never been cited as a book with anything interesting to say about politics and/or political identities; it is basically taken as a book about ritual and emotion.

And what about this book? Let me return to Chapter 2 and my discussion of decision making in Angang. The people I described in that chapter were 'just' taking one-off decisions about potentially risky fishing trips. I suggested that one of the many cultural-historical artefacts to be found in the cognitive environment of Angang may have had some – possibly marginal – impact on the outcome in a couple of cases. But the point I was getting at was actually intended as a much larger point: that the economic psychology of humans in general is *always* heavily impacted by cultural-historical artefacts, including those specifically in the domains of kinship and religion. This can be important for one-off decisions, obviously, but it is actually consequential for everything we do, such as how we live in cooperative (or non-cooperative) communities, the extent to which we accept (or reject) the circumstances in which we are living today and how we take on new ideas about how we might be able to live and about the future possibilities in our lives. Or take the case of Chapter 4 and my discussion of life planning and learning from life in South Bridge. The Chens, the couple I described, were 'just' running a small tea and ices stand in front of a local temple, while their son studied law at university. If one sits with them at their stand in the early evening, which can be very pleasant, you might not think anything political is going on. And yet the broader life decisions of this couple, including in relation to fertility and human capital, have (at the aggregate level) major consequences for political economy over time – as even rationalist economists such as Robert Lucas have recognised. Or take the case from Western Cliff that I discussed in Chapter 5, the one on self-education. The couple I described in that case, the Songs, were 'just' trying to get through life, e.g. by engaging in some entrepreneurial activities with business partners in the period of China's economic reforms and opening-up, when the country was moving away from decades of collectivism. But as an aspect of this, and also as an aspect of family life, they have no choice but to struggle – ceaselessly – with the ethics of cooperation. And this is not just a case of them (individually) learning from life and engaging in a process of personal development, although it is that as well. As Marx (and Hegel) recognised, the process of self-education for the Songs, when viewed at the aggregate level, is a central aspect of the political history of China, and moreover of the human species.

But let me step back and return to the framing I used earlier. Assuming that my intention with these three books – that is, the ones about childhood, about separation and reunion, and about economic psychology – has been to say something concerning politics or political economy, perhaps I made a mistake in writing texts that have had too much to say about kinship and religion, not to mention ones that contain quite a lot of information about the everyday activities of children, their mothers and fathers, their teachers and so on. And although anthropologists are supposed to be the human scientists who – in the spirit of substantivism and holism – do *not* detach kinship and religion from the domains of politics and economics, in practice I would say that they sometimes do.

Speaking honestly, I appear to have a preference, in my writing, for not stating too loudly what my point is. So it is undoubtedly my own fault, to some extent, that these books have not been read as being political. I would just add that the people I've met during fieldwork in rural China and Taiwan often behave in ways that have clear political implications – at least as I see things – but then they don't speak very loudly about this, either. They are 'just' living, as a result of which it might seem that politics is happening somewhere else, and being done by more important people who also care more about explicitly asserting their place in history.

* * *

The problem of human self-education can be approached in a normative way or an empirical way. If we take a normative approach, we are basically asking what kind of outcome from the process of self-education humans *should* have, and this could only be reasonably asked on the basis of us holding some normative view of things. By contrast, if we take an empirical approach, we are 'simply' asking what kind of outcome from the process of self-education humans living in a given set of conditions *do* have. So, for example, if one compares self-education in China and Taiwan, the goal would not be to figure out whether the former is preferable to the latter, or vice versa, but rather to describe and explain the ways in which they differ from each other. As an (empiricist) anthropologist of learning and cognition, I'm definitely interested in the empirical question of self-education, not the normative one. What do these people actually learn? As a human being, however, I'm very interested in the normative question too. In particular, I'm genuinely interested in the question – which I take to be an equally Marxist and Utilitarian question – of whether people have meaningful and self-aware lives in which things go well for them and those they care about. And of course the Marxist claim is not just that people *should* be able to achieve self-education through economic agency (a normative statement), but also that under capitalism they do *not* have the potential to do so (an empirical statement).

The people I've met in China and Taiwan certainly engage in a process of self-education about the cooperative species essence that all humans share. They actually *do* become knowledgeable in this way, but this does not mean that they are able to escape from our species essence itself, and from the ethical dilemmas this generates. As noted in the Preface, when I was carrying out my first period of fieldwork in Taiwan in the mid-1980s, at a time when Taiwan was deeply integrated into global markets, it was still just about possible to refer to China as an example of 'communism'. As everyone knows, however, describing China as communist in any meaningful sense has become increasingly difficult with the passing years. And although Taiwan embraced Western-style capitalism in the early post–civil war decades of the 1950s and 1960s, the backstory to this was also complicated. During the period when the presumed economic 'miracle' was unfolding there, one actually found a form of state corporatism along with a de facto Leninist system of party organisation within factories (Ho 2006). In fact, the KMT's ownership of 'party enterprises' in Taiwan is a truly fascinating story in itself, and one that has had very significant and long-term economic and political implications (Xu 1997).

But let me frame this from the vantage point of someone who did anthropological fieldwork in Taiwan and China in the mid-1980s and afterwards. While the middle-aged and older people I met during fieldwork in China had lived through some stages of high Maoism, they had also subsequently lived through the arrival of Deng's economic reforms and all that followed from that. By the time I arrived in Dragon Head, in north-east China, this was quite a particular type of communism to be living under – 'socialism with Chinese characteristics', as the saying had it. Meanwhile, the middle-aged and older people I met during fieldwork in Taiwan had lived through the so-called miracle there, and this – as just noted – entailed living through quite a particular form of capitalism. In the ensuing years, in fact, by far the most important factor in the type of capitalism experienced by people in Taiwan was the political-economic situation across the strait in notionally communist China.

Against this background, would it make any sense to argue that self-education in the Taiwanese community of South Bridge, at the time of my fieldwork there, was being *impeded* by the Taiwanese version of capitalism? Could one argue that self-education in the Chinese community of Protected Mountain, at the time of my fieldwork there, was being *enabled* by the Chinese version of communism? To me, these are basically unanswerable questions, not least because of the rapidly shifting political-economic landscape of these two places. But they are nonetheless interesting questions, in my view, i.e. because of what was simultaneously going on at the level of the (also rapidly shifting) politics of cultural tradition in these two places. To return to what I have said earlier, if we think of self-education as a function not only of economics and politics but also of kinship and religion – as I firmly believe we should – a further layer of complexity is added to the comparison of self-education in China and Taiwan.

Of course, making comparisons of any kind between China and Taiwan is already difficult, and highly politicised. From China's perspective, Taiwan is a renegade province that it definitely intends to reunite with. If certain features of life can be said to be 'the same' on both sides of the strait, this is proof that they do indeed share a common Chinese culture and identity. Opinions in Taiwan are famously divided between those who explicitly advocate independence (on the basis that Taiwan is *not* China), those who reject independence as a viable option – be this on ideological or pragmatic grounds – and those who sit in the middle. Taiwan has been a seemingly modern place for decades – at least, very Western-oriented and comfortable with this. But a key point to bear in mind is that it is also arguably more *traditional* than China in the particular sense that it held onto (and to some extent nurtured for political purposes) aspects of traditional kinship and religious practices that in mainland China came under fierce attack during the revolutionary era. Meanwhile, however, these revolutionary attempts to defeat 'feudal ways of thinking' in China have had a mixed track record – with many of the long-term consequences yet to be realised. To give a prominent example, China's evolving family-planning policy (the so-called one-child policy) has, without doubt, introduced huge changes in family life and kinship, and many people in China would say that it has effectively killed tradition. Along the way, however, it has arguably made ordinary Chinese people care more than ever about reproducing the family line, leading them to be more fervent than ever about Confucian ideals, including those surrounding the importance of education for their children. As I have suggested elsewhere, Confucius himself could probably never have imagined the extent to which the worship of the family and of education would take off in modern China ... after decades of Maoist anti-traditionalism.[3]

It can also be argued that China, having gone through a failed experiment in cooperative living, has now adopted a more extreme type of capitalism than is to be found in Taiwan, one characterised by huge social disruption with limited state aid for the less fortunate *and* characterised as well by the absence (except in weakened form) of 'traditional' social mechanisms for binding people into supportive social groups. Of course, this transformation has also lifted many millions of people out of poverty. And my own experience, in the Chinese countryside, has been that traditional social mechanisms are still a major fact of life for many people – in spite of all the disruptions – and in particular that such things as gift-exchange networks and kinship ties, as well as religion to some extent, continue to play an important role in sustaining sociality, however transformed they may have been (Oxfeld 2010, Yan 1996). Indeed, as I noted in the case of Protected Mountain, the reform era has seen a resurgence of tradition in many locations – rebuilding of ancestral temples and so on. Meanwhile, most people in Taiwan arguably experienced a relatively benign type of capitalism, one in which income inequality did not get dramatically out of hand (helped, in the early years, by a major land reform), and one in which traditional or quasi-traditional social mechanisms for binding people into social

---

[3] Stafford (2011b).

groups remained largely in place, even while being transformed in history. This era also left Taiwan relatively wealthy in global terms, and certainly very significantly wealthier on a per capita basis than China is, even today, after four decades of economic reforms and opening up. A not insignificant proportion of this wealth has been re-invested in 'tradition', as I explained in Chapter 4.

But here let me use the terminology of the economic anthropologist James Carrier to try to characterise what I have experienced. The particular Taiwanese communities *and* the particular Chinese communities where I have carried out fieldwork did not appear to me, at the time I studied them, to have been very far along the path of 'emerging alienation' that might be assumed to accompany the arrival of modern capitalism (Carrier 1992). At least at the time of my fieldwork, in other words, these communities were in an in-between space; this is actually something that all of the communities I have studied share, notwithstanding the differences between the political economies of China and Taiwan, and notwithstanding the differences between my five fieldsites. In Marxist terms, this means that the people in these communities should, at least in theory, have been in a position to actually achieve self-education through cooperative economic agency; that is, this process should not have been entirely blocked. And yet, as I have suggested in Chapter 5, they might instead be said to be trapped or enchanted by the *human species* essence itself, from which no history will let them escape. Of course, the standard Marxist understanding is that kinship ideals and (especially) religious beliefs, may have the function precisely of *hiding* the extent to which political and economic relations are exploitative. Believing in the gods, for example, is a way of wrongly imagining our own productive capacities to be those of the gods instead (whereas they aren't) and/or of wrongly imagining that our reward is going to be in heaven (whereas it won't). In the particular cases of Taiwan and China, it would be easier to accept this account were it not so obviously the case that popular religion has been a vehicle for popular resistance – be it against the Confucian ideologues, the Japanese, the KMT or the communists.[4] For this reason, and further to Carrier, I would argue that kinship and religion in the particular cases of rural China and Taiwan are *not* performing, or at least not fully performing, the ideological function that hypothetically might be ascribed to them under full-blown capitalism. That is, people there do still share a genuinely cooperative form of life – one that individuals can learn from, at least to some extent, as part of the process of self-education in the flow of history. The problem, as I have explained, isn't so much that kinship and religion are ideological in the service of political economy, although they may be this as well, but rather that they are, at least to some extent, ideological in the service of kinship and religion themselves.

[4] See Feuchtwang (2001).

SEVEN

Number and Structure

I began the Introduction with a brief story from Protected Mountain, in far south-western China. As I explained, this community has had a very interesting economic history, one in which fortunes (at least by local standards) were made in the pre-revolutionary era through work and trade in nearby Burma. One day during my stay in Protected Mountain, as I mentioned, a friend and I came upon two children who were selling bananas in front of the Temple of Learning. After some back and forth, we made a purchase from them and the exchange ended on congenial terms, with my friend giving the children some helpful advice about handling sales transactions and dealing with customers. I used the story to illustrate two basic points that underpin this book as a whole: (a) that economic life is intrinsically psychological (e.g. it involves cognitive skills such as numeracy) and (b) that economic psychology is intrinsically cultural-historical (e.g. schooling does not come in the same form in all human societies, nor is its existence a universal given).

As it happens, the two children we met on that day did not appear to be especially skilled at calculation – at least not during the course of our transaction with them. My friend had to tell them how much to charge us. But to the extent that they *were* numerate, a range of social/cultural/ historical factors will have played some role in this. Indeed, even totally innumerate people in China are bound to be influenced by the Chinese 'culture of numbers' that pervades the cognitive environments in which they live, and which I will discuss more fully further on. I concluded by saying that my story about the passing encounter is directly linked to the much longer story that can be told about this community, i.e. the story of its economic rise and fall over time.

I didn't spell out what I meant by this, but let me do so now. In Protected Mountain, 'economy' and 'learning' have long had a complex, symbiotic relationship. A key point is that many locals hold what could be described as an explicitly Confucian outlook on the world. They stress the virtues of filial piety and family loyalty. At the time of my fieldwork, they were putting a lot of money and effort into holding elaborate family rituals, especially large-scale funerals, and in refurbishing ancestral halls. Moreover, they seemed very committed, at least at the level of discourse, to the Confucian ideal of pursuing education and self-cultivation. For example, I met people there who styled themselves as 'calligraphers', which is perhaps surprising given that this was a rural area where one would not normally expect to find high levels of cultural achievement. But the whole point is that Protected Mountain *is* a place where education and cultural achievement are prioritised, or so many local people will tell you. For visitors arriving from the outside, the most visible temple, and the place where we met the two children, is the Temple of Learning (*wenmiao*). Very near to this stands an impressive building I didn't mention in the Introduction: an old wood-framed library – again, a rather unusual sight in a place of this kind, surrounded by fields and farmhouses.

So, how was it that these cultural-historical artefacts of 'learning', these institutions, came to exist – and moreover so prominently – in Protected Mountain? The simple answer is that they are there because of what had happened in the local economy. Prosperous Chinese sojourners (*huaqiao*) who had left Protected Mountain for Burma then re-invested some of the wealth they earned back into their native community, i.e. on the Chinese side of the border. This came not only via direct support for their own relatives but also via business investments *and* contributions to the public good. They felt that this was, among other things, a way of bringing glory to their ancestors.

As anthropologists would expect, however, the reality behind this inspiring tale of success-turned-into-good-works is accompanied by some twists and turns. One point, which I won't dwell on here, is that the prototypically 'Chinese' and 'Confucian' orientation of this community is in part a function of its marginality. As noted, Protected Mountain is near the China-Burma border. This is an ethnically mixed region, and there has been a significant amount of intermarriage with non-Han. One might conclude that the people in this place have actually felt the need to express (even advertise) their Chineseness, before anybody could think of challenging it. In any case, the Revolution, when it came, had dramatic consequences, not only in practical terms but also in relation to local identities. The border was closed, and there was a decades-long period during which Confucian-style traditionalism and 'learning' in general – the foundation of Chineseness, as this had formerly been understood by residents of Protected Mountain – came under explicit criticism and, at times, direct assault. Especially during the Cultural Revolution, to practise calligraphy was suspect, to have ornate flourishes on one's home was suspect, to worship the ancestors (at least publically) was simply forbidden.

Such practices have been re-validated in the post-Mao era of economic reform, as has been the practice of maintaining ties with overseas relatives and engaging in overseas business. But this process of re-validation has been uneven. The investments of various kinds that Chinese *huaqiao* have made in communities such as Protected Mountain, however welcome on the whole, have not been uncontroversial. The rewards are distributed unequally, and in fact *huaqiao* activity often creates a good deal of tension and resentment in local communities. The wider post-Mao economic boom has also had uneven consequences, of course, with its rewards distributed unequally. Especially in rural areas, we find millions who have been 'left behind' in some way, famously including the children of migrant workers who are looked after by their grandparents or others.

The two children we met in front of the Temple of Learning should have been in school on that weekday. But not all families can afford the fees and charges that go along with this, and not all children actually do stay in school. These two children were likely to have been from a more remote, and relatively poor, village outside of Protected Mountain proper – the kind of place where schooling is less of a priority (on the grounds, in at least some cases, that 'our' children can never succeed in the intense competition that modern Chinese schooling entails). Perhaps they were looked after by grandparents or other elders, who can sometimes have very different ideas from their juniors about the transformative potential of schooling. In any case, I didn't see these children again, and in fact I have no evidence about the actual circumstances in which they lived. All I know for sure is that they weren't in school when they should have been, and that they stumbled a bit when calculating the price of bananas. There is definitely a history to both of these facts – if you like, to both the cognitive one and the social one. And the point I am getting at is that the two histories are interlinked.

* * *

If economists were asked to name a cognitive skill – a type of human capital – that really matters for economic life, then numeracy would presumably be among the top contenders. The connection to economic agency is obvious. Certainly, much of modern economic life is 'numerical' in a direct sense. Prices are rendered numerically, which means that in buying things we're obliged to think in numbers at least to some extent. Is it a good idea to purchase more packs of paper than we actually need because at bulk it's sold at a lower price? The answer could be tricky, but knowing the actual numbers (e.g. the amount of money we could save per pack) would help. If we need to argue with someone over price – that is, if we want to haggle – we have to think, and talk, in numbers. And if we are selling something, we might need to be able to count out the change. Even at this very basic level, numeracy is important for effective participation in economic life. But there's more. The packs (or boxes) of paper we eventually buy are likely to have a barcode on them, which is one way of displaying numerical information. We'll ignore this. But it is a modern (and IT-friendly) version of an old idea: it's part of a system for tracking goods so that production, distribution and sales can be properly *accounted* for. Buyers, sellers, workers, bosses and accountants all need to know – to varying degrees – their numbers. Some individuals can be innumerate and get by, of course, and much of the work being done by numbers in modern societies goes unnoticed (e.g. as in the case of barcodes). But a basic level of numeracy is presumably an economically useful component of the human capital of a given population.

Indeed, the argument for the significance of numeracy and quantification in modern economic life can be taken a step further. Many of the key practices around which the global economy is built – engineering, chemistry, information technology and so on – are 'numerical' or 'mathematical' in a deep sense. It sometimes feels as if quantifiability is the sine qua non, which is one of the reasons that parents in East Asia are generally keen on their children receiving a good education in maths. Not every doctor, scientist or software programmer has to be a good mathematician, of course. And numeracy does not translate, just like that, into economic success – or even into a job. But all things being equal, a high level of numerical/mathematical literacy in a given population would be presumed, by most, to be a positive thing. Mathematical literacy prepares some people in this population, some of the time, for a life in trade, technology or science. And it arguably makes it more likely, statistically, that this population will produce economically useful knowledge – thus generating some knowledge externalities. As a result, even economists who wanted to adopt a rather restricted definition of economics-relevant learning (in other words, who wanted to keep the concept of human capital as simple as possible) would likely allow numeracy into the frame.

But how best to study this topic if we want to go deeper into it? As I mentioned in a previous chapter, we can draw on the extensive interdisciplinary literature that focuses on how humans master basic numerical skills and eventually put them to use in the world. Unfortunately, however, numerical cognition turns out to be a very challenging topic – not least because 'number' itself is philosophically challenging. A plausible account of numeracy has to address not only the neurophysiology of the evolved human brain, but the domain-specificity of human thinking about number, not to mention the wide range of cultural-historical artefacts – everything from counting terms to national pedagogical systems – that mediate numerical cognition in everyday life contexts. (For an accessible and engaging introduction that brings much of this together, see Dehaene 1999.)

* * *

In a series of articles, I've discussed numerical thought and number use among 'ordinary people' in the 'real-world' contexts I've studied during fieldwork in rural China and Taiwan (Stafford 2003, 2004, 2007, 2008b, 2009, 2010a, 2012). Of course, China and Taiwan, being embedded in the global market economy, are number-oriented in all the ways I've mentioned earlier. Mathematics is a central part of modern schooling there, to be sure, and there are many ways in which quantification impinges on everyday economic life, ranging from everyday buying and selling transactions to the organisation of industry. But in the case of China and Taiwan, there is something else. We also find a highly elaborate 'culture of numbers' that is a central element in the folk understanding of reality.

To give an example that might at first seem minor but isn't, most Chinese families post poetic couplets around their front door frames as part of the New Year celebrations, and these often contain numbers. In Protected Mountain, for instance, I saw this one displayed on a door frame: 'The five flavours exquisitely blended in the kitchen! The three relations gathered before the ancestors!' (The five flavours are sour, sweet, bitter, spicy, salty; the three relations are husband-wife, father-son, brother-brother.) Most people wouldn't pay that much attention to individual poetic couplets of these kinds. They're background noise, essentially, and convey highly conventional sentiments, e.g. about the family, about the desire for prosperity, etc. But they nicely illustrate a pervasive Chinese cultural tendency, which is to render experience numerically – if you like, to say things with numbers. To give a less traditional-sounding illustration of this tendency, in 2000, actually just before I went to Dragon Head, the Chinese leader Jiang Zemin put forward a widely publicised and discussed political theory called 'The Three Represents'; it is absolutely typical, in the case of China, that political theories, programmes and policies should come in numbered lists of this kind. For example, China's rural welfare system has specified that highly vulnerable households should receive support for food, clothing, fuel, education and burial expenses; thus are they labelled the 'Five-Guarantee Households'. Examples along these lines are endless.

Meanwhile, during my periods of fieldwork in rural Taiwan, an especially salient form of number-related activity revolved around the lottery. The people I met were incredibly keen participants in this (illegal) lottery, and they invested a significant amount of time and trouble in coming up with numbers for it. Sometimes they did this in a rather casual way in the flow of everyday life. For example, they would happen to spot numbers on a motorcycle license plate or on the side of a cardboard box sitting on the street outside of a betel nut shop. Then they would think about entering those numbers into the lottery. Sometimes they went to spirit-medium altars in order to try to find good lottery numbers, which they might actually 'read' in the incense smoke floating over a god's statue – taking this as a friendly steer from a benevolent spirit.

This example of lottery numbers and divination practices relates to a broader point that can be made about China's culture of numbers, which is that popular ideas about fate and fortune play an essential role in it. This is a complex topic, which I will not address in detail here. But put simply, Chinese cosmology (i.e. Chinese ideas about the nature of universe and how everything in it works) is in general terms very numerological in orientation. As an extension of this, a high proportion of fortune telling and divination is also explicitly numerological in orientation. Fortune tellers are asked to literally 'calculate fate' (*suanming*) for their clients, normally in relation to astrological reckonings that bring individual circumstances together with the machinations of the universe as a whole. Most ordinary people don't understand the system behind this, and they don't care greatly about the details. But they *do* understand that the patterns of the universe can be rendered numerically and that one's fate can therefore be 'calculated' by a specialist. One interesting way of doing so focuses on the brushstrokes in names. These are added up – bearing in mind that Chinese dictionaries are typically organised according to a numerical logic, on a brushstroke-count basis. An analysis can then be carried out in which the brushstroke count of an individual's full name is related back to the date and time of his or her birth. If it is felt necessary, the name itself – and thus the calculation of the brushstrokes – can be changed in order (a) to come up with a more auspicious stroke-count sum and/or (b) to incorporate into the written name one or more of the Five Elements (such as 'earth'), if this is felt to be lacking in the original name and to be causing problems for the person in question.

As the last point about the Five Elements illustrates, this cosmology is not just a numerical one in a crude sense – it's more complicated than that. What it is ultimately about is the fact that the universe (and within that, human experience, along with the natural environments in which human experience takes place) is a thing of patterns and structures. Number can help us grasp and communicate about these patterns and structures; but the deeper logic is always a structural one – it's about relations. The numerical poetry posted around door frames in Protected

Mountain during New Year festivities provides one (very simplified) illustration of this. On the one hand, as I've said, there are some numbers to be found in the couplet itself: 'the three relations', and so on. But there is also a *structural* relationship between the two poetic phrases which are posted on the right and left sides of the door, respectively, and which are matched. That is, we find the same number of characters and also a degree of poetic coupling of the sentiments and even the individual characters in the two lines (e.g. 'the three relations' are matched with 'the five flavours'). In regulated Chinese classical poetry, this sort of logic is taken further, e.g. because the spoken *tonality* of the characters in the lines (Chinese being a tonal language) is also matched. The extent of the structural constraint imposed on poets by all of this – and within which they are meant to express their creativity – is basically the whole point of the exercise.

Of course, most people aren't specialists at poetry, and nor do they claim to understand cosmology in the manner of the experts; they aren't poets, diviners or philosophers. However, they *do* have an interest in numbers and numerology, to be sure. They understand that life is fateful and that one of the reasons for being interested in number is that it might help you control, to some extent, what happens in the course of your life. In other words, numerical thought is not only about helping you grasp what is going on around you; it is also a way of helping you change what is going on around you. As I have already explained, however, there are actually two very different (if ultimately interconnected) ways of controlling fate in the Chinese countryside. One entails the kind of cosmological thinking I have just been referring to. To put it simply, this is about using numerological/structural approaches as a way not only of understanding the universe but also – where possible – of tinkering around to see if you might be able to improve life outcomes for yourself and those you care about. The other approach is more grounded in everyday human relations: it is about developing the kind of connections with others that you need to have in order to ensure that a particular kind of (good) future is the one that you end up with. A key point to bear in mind, however, is that just as the universe has its patterns, so too do human relations have theirs. And in the Chinese case, at least, a key consideration is the pattern of 'separations' and 'reunions' that mark our kin and non-kin relationships in the real world. By handling these processes properly and effectively, including via rituals, we can in effect create a future for ourselves – one in which the people (and spirits) we depend on will be more likely to be there for us into the future. And while the cosmological approach is more explicitly numerological, the relational approach – being structural – can also itself be said to be mathematical (Stafford 2007). At the same time, both of these approaches are psychological. The mathematical way of seeing the world is a complex elaboration of the evolved 'number sense' that all humans share, and the relational way of seeing the world is a complex elaboration of the evolved psychology of attachment and of cooperation that all humans share.

* * *

Many anthropologists (and most students of anthropology, in my experience) are resistant to quantification. More specifically, many of them think of number as the starting point for objectivism and crude reductionism. So, if I tell anthropologists that people in China are very interested in numbers, this is something they might actually hold against them, I would guess. What they somewhat miss, I think, is an important ethnographic reality: that for many ordinary people (and not only in China) there is something creative and potentially magical about the world of numbers (Guyer et al. 2010). Using numerological thought is not just about number crunching in a reductionist sense. On the contrary, what we actually see in Chinese folk practice is a kind of 'qualitative mathematics' that is highly imaginative (Stafford 2010a). Of course, one of the truisms of anthropology is that we should pay attention to what our fieldwork interlocutors think, and take it seriously.

I now see that while having an interest in thinking via numbers and structural patterns is – without doubt – an attempt at simplification, it is also at least somewhat poetic. Among other things, it opens up complex and interesting questions about the nature of human experience. This folk qualitative mathematics is not, in fact, unrelated to the way in which economists set about doing their work. Just as thinking in a highly structured way is helpful to ordinary people in China and Taiwan, so it can be to economists. Similarly, there is a folk *psychology* in China, heavily oriented to the problems of intention-reading and cooperation, that overlaps in many important respects with exactly the topics that psychologists of cooperation have been studying in recent years.

An economist might say that the problem with anthropologists is that by getting so interested in 'real-life' stories they fail to see the structural patterns that are staring them in the face – or, at least, that are discoverable if they worked hard enough on the underlying data. In reply, an anthropologist might say that the further we get from the everyday experiences of ordinary people the more we risk losing track of what is really going on at the human level – which, in the end, is what really matters. (Note that most economists would presumably not agree with this characterisation of what really matters for the human sciences.) As I said in the Preface, I would like to bring anthropology, psychology and economics into a closer conversation. But this doesn't mean that we have to give up being critical of each other. So far as I know, the reason economists ignore anthropology isn't that they disagree with it on normative grounds. At the level of aggregation economists actually want to focus on, ethnographic data is not normally very useful: it just can't answer the questions that economists are asking. By contrast, a number of economists have considered psychology serious enough to merit a full engagement – so much so that some of them have actually turned themselves into psychologists (of a kind). The same thing is not happening among the anthropologists: i.e. very few of us are turning ourselves into psychologists, for the reasons I have explained. I personally think that the anthropological critique of psychology could actually have a lot more traction, in the end, than the anthropological critique of economics. The problem is that if psychologists were to take anthropology seriously – that is, if they were to take the cultural-historical critique of psychology seriously – it would represent a major change in disciplinary outlook and practice. As for anthropologists taking psychology seriously – which would also represent a major change in disciplinary outlook and practice – I hope this book will have made at least a modest contribution to that.

References

Amsden, Alice (2001), *The Rise of the Rest*, Oxford: Oxford University Press.

Angrist, Joshua & Jörn-Steffen Pischke (2009), *Mostly Harmless Econometrics: An Empiricist's Companion*, Princeton: Princeton University Press.

Appadurai, Arjun (1996), *Modernity at Large: Cultural Dimensions of Globalization*, Minneapolis: University of Minnesota Press.

Argote, Linda & Dennis Epple (1990), Learning curves in manufacturing, *Science* (n.s.) 247(4945):920–4.

Ariely, Dan (2008), *Predictably Irrational: The Hidden Forces That Shape Our Decisions*, New York: HarperCollins.

Astuti, Rita (2007), What happens after death? In R. Astuti, J. Parry & C. Stafford (eds.), *Questions of Anthropology*. London School of Economics Monographs on Social Anthropology, no. 76. Oxford: Berg, pp. 227–47.

Astuti, Rita, Greg Solomon & Susan Carey (2004), Constraints on conceptual development: A case study of the acquisition of folkbiological and folksociological knowledge in Madagascar, *Monographs of the Society for Research in Child Development* 69(277): 3.

Barth, Fredrik (1967), On the study of social change, *American Anthropologist* 69: 661–9.

Baumard, Nicolas, Jean-Baptiste Andre & Dan Sperber (2013), A mutualistic approach to morality: The evolution of fairness by partner choice, *Behavioral and Brain Sciences* 36: 59–122.

Becker, Gary (1993a), The economic way of looking at life. Coase-Sandor Institute for Law and Economics Working Paper Number 12.

(1993b), *A Treatise on the Family*, Enlarged edition, Cambridge, MA: Harvard University Press.

Bloch, Maurice (1998), *How We Think They Think: Anthropological Studies in Cognition, Memory and Literacy*, Boulder: Westview Press.

References

(2005), *Essays on Cultural Transmission*, Oxford: Berg.

(2012), *Anthropology and the Cognitive Challenge*, Cambridge: Cambridge University Press.

(2013), *In and Out of Each Other's Bodies: Theories of Mind, Evolution, Truth, and the Nature of the Social*, London: Routledge.

Boden, Margaret A. (2006), *Mind as Machine: A History of Cognitive Science*, Volumes 1 & 2, Oxford: Clarendon Press.

Bowlby, John (1980), *Attachment and Loss, Volume 3, Loss: Sadness and Depression*. New York: Basic Books.

Bowles, Samuel & Herbert Gintis (2011), *A Cooperative Species: Human Reciprocity and Its Evolution*, Princeton: Princeton University Press.

Bray, Francesca (1997), *Technology and Gender: Fabrics of Power in Late Imperial China*, Berkeley: University of California Press.

Bruni, Luigino & Robert Sugden (2007), The road not taken: How psychology was removed from economics, and how it might be brought back, *The Economic Journal* 117: 146–73.

Burawoy, Michael (2003), For a sociological Marxism: The complementary convergence of Antonio Gramsci and Karl Polanyi, *Politics and Society* 31(2): 193–261.

Camerer, Colin, George Lowenstein & Drazen Prelec (2005), Neuroeconomics: How neuroscience can inform economics. *Journal of Economic Literature* 43(1): 9–64.

Carrier, James (1992), Emerging alienation in production: A Maussian history, *Man* 27(3): 539–58.

(2005), *A Handbook of Economic Anthropology*, Cheltenham: Edward Elgar.

Chibnik, Michael (1980), Working out or working in: The choice between wage labor and cash cropping in rural Belize, *American Ethnologist* 7(1): 86–105.

(2005), Experimental economics in anthropology, *American Ethnologist* 32(2): 198–209.

(2011), *Anthropology, Economics, and Choice*, Austin: University of Texas Press.

Chomsky, Noam (1996), *Class Warfare*, London: Pluto Press.

Da Col, Giovanni & Caroline Humphrey (2012), Cosmologies of fortune: Luck, vitality and uncontrolled vitality, *Social Analysis* (Special issue) 62(1): 1–23.

Damasio, Antonio (2006 [1994]), *Descartes' Error: Emotion, Reason and the Human Brain*, London: Vintage.

Davies, William (2011), The political economy of unhappiness, *New Left Review* 71: 65–80.

Davis, Deborah & Stevan Harrell (eds.) (1993), *Chinese Families in the Post-Mao Era*, Berkeley: University of California Press.

Dehaene, Stanislas (1997), *The Number Sense: How the Mind Creates Mathematics*, Oxford: Oxford University Press.

References

(1999), *The Number Sense: How the Mind Creates Mathematics*, London, UK: Penguin.

Dietrich, Franz & Christian List (2012), Where do preferences come from? *International Journal of Game Theory*, 42(3): 613–37.

Dunn, Barnaby D., Tim Dalgleish & Andrew D. Lawrence (2006), The somatic marker hypothesis: A critical evaluation, *Neuroscience and Biobehavioral Reviews* 30: 239–71.

Earle, Joe, Cahal Moran & Zach Ward-Perkins (2016), *The Econocracy: The Perils of Leaving Economics to the Experts*, Manchester: Manchester University Press.

Easterly, William (2001), *The Elusive Quest for Growth*, Boston: MIT Press.

Elliott, Alan J. A. (1955), *Chinese Spirit-Medium Cults in Singapore*, London School of Economics Monographs on Social Anthropology, No. 14, London: Athlone.

Fei, Xiaotong (1939), *Peasant Life in China*, London: Routledge.

Ferguson, James (1985), The bovine mystique: Power, property and livestock in rural Lesotho, *Man* 20(4): 647–74.

Feuchtwang, Stephan (2001), *Chinese Popular Religion: The Imperial Metaphor*, Richmond: Curzon Press.

Friedman, Milton (1966), *Essays in Positive Economics*, Chicago: University of Chicago Press.

Fuller, Chris (2004), *The Renewal of the Priesthood: Modernity and Traditionalism in a South Indian Temple*, Princeton: Princeton University Press.

Gates, Hill (1996), *China's Motor: A Thousand Years of Petty Capitalism*, Ithaca: Cornell University Press.

Gigerenzer, Gerd (2000), *Adaptive Thinking: Rationality in the Real World*, Oxford: Oxford University Press.

(2007), *Gut Feelings: Short Cuts to Better Decision Making*, London: Penguin.

(2008), *Rationality for Mortals: How People Cope with Uncertainty*, Oxford: Oxford University Press.

Granovetter, Mark (1974/1995), *Getting a Job: A Study of Contacts and Careers*, Second edition, Chicago: University of Chicago Press.

(1985), Economic action and social structure: The problem of embeddedness, *American Journal of Sociology* 91(3): 481–510.

Guala, Francesco (2012), Reciprocity: Weak or strong? What punishment experiments do (and do not) demonstrate, *Behavioral and Brain Sciences* 35(1): 1–59.

Gul, Faruk & Wolfgang Pesendorfer (2008), The case for mindless economics, in Andrew Caplan & Andrew Shotter (eds.), *The Foundations of Positive and Normative Economics*, Oxford: Oxford University Press.

Guyer, Jane et al. (2010), Introduction: Number as inventive frontier, *Anthropological Theory* 10(1–2): 36–61.

Hann, Chris & Keith Hart (2011), *Economic Anthropology*, Cambridge: Polity Press.

Harris, Paul (2012), *Trusting What You're Told: How Children Learn from Others*, Cambridge, MA: Harvard University Press.

Heath, Joseph (2015), Methodological individualism, in Edward N. Zalta (ed.), *The Stanford Encyclopaedia of Philosophy*, Spring 2015 edition. https://plato.stanford.edu/cgi-bin/encyclopedia/archinfo.cgi?entry= methodological-individualism.

Henrich, Joseph et al. (2004), *Foundations of Human Sociality: Economic Experiments and Ethnographic Evidence from Fifteen Small-Scale Societies*, Oxford: Oxford University Press.

Hirschfeld, Lawrence (1998), *Race in the Making: Cognition, Culture, and the Child's Construction of Human Kinds*, Cambridge, MA: MIT Press.

Ho, Ming-sho (2006), Challenging state corporatism: The politics of Taiwan's labor federation movement, *The China Journal* 56: 107–27.

Hrdy, Sarah Blaffer (2011), *Mothers and Others: The Evolutionary Origins of Mutual Understanding*, Cambridge, MA: Harvard University Press.

Huang, Yasheng (2008), *Capitalism with Chinese Characteristics: Entrepreneurship and the State*, Cambridge: Cambridge University Press.

Hutchins, Edwin (1995), *Cognition in the Wild*, Cambridge, MA: MIT Press.

Inda, Jonathan Xavier & Renata Rosaldo (2008), *The Anthropology of Globalization: A Reader*, Second edition, Oxford: Blackwell Publishers.

Ingold, Tim (2000), *The Perception of the Environment: Essays on Livelihood, Dwelling and Skill*, London: Routledge.

Jacobs, Jane (1984), *Cities and the Wealth of Nations*, New York: Random House.

Janssen, Maarten (1993), *Microfoundations: A Critical Inquiry*, London: Routledge.

(2008), Microfoundations, in Steven N. Durlauf & Lawrence E. Blume (eds.), *The New Palgrave Dictionary of Economics*, Second Edition, London: Palgrave Macmillan.

Johnson, Dominic (2016), *God Is Watching You: How the Fear of God Makes Us Human*, Oxford: Oxford University Press.

Jordan, David (1972), *Gods, Ghosts and Ancestors: Folk Religion in a Taiwanese Village*. Berkeley: University of California Press.

Jordan, David K. & Daniel L. Overmyer (1986), *The Flying Phoenix: Aspects of Chinese Sectarianism in Taiwan*, Princeton: Princeton University Press.

Kahneman, Daniel (2003), A psychological perspective on economics, *The American Economic Review* 93(2): 162–8.

(2011), *Thinking Fast and Slow*, New York: Farrar, Straus and Giroux.

References

Kahneman, Daniel & Amos Tversky (eds.) (2000), *Choices, Values and Frames*, Cambridge: Cambridge University Press.

Knight, Frank (1921), *Risk, Uncertainty and Profit*, Boston: Houghton Mifflin.

Kolakowski, Leszek (1978/2005), *Main Currents of Marxism* (three volumes), Oxford: Oxford University Press.

Konnor, Melvin (2011), It does take a village, New York Review of Books, 8 December 2011.

Kurz, Heinz D. (2016), *Economic Thought: A Brief History*, New York: Columbia University Press.

Laidlaw, James (2013), *The Subject of Virtue: An Anthropology of Ethics and Freedom*, Cambridge: Cambridge University Press.

Langlois, Richard N. & Metin M. Cosgell (1993), Frank Knight on risk, uncertainty, and the firm: A new interpretation, *Economic Inquiry* 31: 456–65.

Lave, Jean (1988), *Cognition in Practice: Mind, Mathematics and Culture in Everyday Life*, Cambridge: Cambridge University Press.

Layard, Richard (2005), *Happiness: Lessons from a New Science*, London: Allen Lane.

Lazear, Edward P. (2000), Economic imperialism, *Quarterly Journal of Economics* 115(1): 99–146.

Levine, Donald N. (2005), The continuing challenge of Weber's theory of rational action, in C. Camic, P. S. Gorski & D. M. Trubek (eds.), *Max Weber's 'Economy and Society'*, Stanford: Stanford University Press, pp. 101–26.

Liu, Xin (2002), *The Otherness of Self: A Genealogy of the Self in Contemporary China*, Ann Arbor: University of Michigan Press.

Lucas, Robert E. (1977), Understanding business cycles, *Carnegie-Rochester Conference Series on Public Policy* 5(1): 7–29.

(1986), Adaptive behavior and economic theory, *Journal of Business* 59(4): S401–26.

(2002), *Lectures on economic growth*, Cambridge, MA: Harvard University Press.

(2011), What economists do, *Journal of Applied Economics* 14(1): 1–4.

Lucas, Robert E. & Edward C. Prescott (1971), Investment under uncertainty, *Econometrica* 39(5): 659–81.

Maas, Harro (2009), Disciplining boundaries: Lionel Robbins, Max Weber, and the borderlands of economics, history, and psychology, *Journal of The History of Economic Thought* 31(4): 500–17.

MacKenzie, Donald (2006), *An Engine, Not a Camera: How Financial Models Shape Markets*, Cambridge, MA: MIT Press.

Marchand, Trevor (2009), *The Masons of Djenne*, Bloomington: Indiana University Press.

(ed.) (2016), *Craftwork as Problem Solving: Ethnographic Studies of Design and Making*, Farnham: Ashgate.

McKinnon, Susan & Fenella Cannell (eds.). (2013), *Vital Relations: Modernity and the Persistent Life of Kinship*, Santa Fe: School for Advanced Research Seminar Series.

Mei-Hui Yang, Mayfair (1994), *Gifts, Favors and Banquets: The Art of Social Relationships in China*, Ithaca: Cornell University Press.

Mercier, Hugo & Dan Sperber (2011), Why do humans reason? Arguments for an argumentative theory, *Behavioral and Brain Sciences* 34: 57–111.

(2017), *The Enigma of Reason: A New Theory of Human Understanding*, London: Allen Lane.

Mitchell, Timothy (2005), The work of economics: How a discipline makes its world, *European Journal of Sociology* 46(2): 297–320.

North, Douglass C. (1995), The new institutional economics and third world development, in John Harriss, Janet Hunter & Colin M. Lewis (eds.), *The New Institutional Economics and Third World Development*, London: Routledge.

Obeyesekere, Gananath (1984), *Medusa's Hair: An Essay on Personal Symbols and Religious Experience*, Chicago: University of Chicago Press.

Öhman, Arne (2006), Making sense of emotion: Evolution, reason & the brain, *Daedalus* 135(3): 33–45.

Ortiz, Sutti (2005), Decisions and choices: The rationality of economic actors, in J. Carrier (ed.), *A Handbook of Economic Anthropology*, Cheltenham: Edward Elgar, pp. 59–77.

Oxfeld, Ellen (2010), *Drink Water but Remember the Source: Moral Discourse in a Chinese Village*, Berkeley: University of California Press.

Parfit, Derek (1984), *Reasons and Persons*, Oxford: Oxford University Press.

(2011), *On What Matters*, Oxford: Oxford University Press.

Pelkmans, Mathijs (2017), *Fragile Conviction: Changing Ideological Landscapes in Urban Kyrgyzstan*, Ithaca: Cornell University Press.

(ed.). (2013), *Ethnographies of Doubt: Faith and Uncertainty in Contemporary Societies*, London: I. B. Tauris.

Persky, Joseph (2016), *The Political Economy of Progress: John Stuart Mill and Modern Radicalism*, Oxford: Oxford University Press.

Pew Research Center (2012), *The Global Religious Landscape: A Report on the Size and Distribution of the World's Major Religious Groups as of 2010*, Washington, DC: Pew Research Center.

Piketty, Thomas (2014), *Capital in the Twenty-First Century*, Cambridge, MA: Harvard University Press.

References

Pippin, Robert B. (2010), *Hegel on Self-Consciousness*, Princeton: Princeton University Press.

Pollak, Robert A. (2002), Gary Becker's contributions to family and household economics. NBER Working Paper 9232.

Post-Crash Economics Society (2014), *Economics, Education and Unlearning*, Manchester: Post-Crash Economics Society.

Poulton, Richie & Ross G. Menzies (2002), Non-associative fear acquisition: A review of the evidence from retrospective and longitudinal research, *Behaviour Research and Therapy* 40: 127–249.

Quinn, Naomi (1978), Do Mfantse fish sellers estimate probabilities in their heads? *American Ethnologist* 5(2): 206–26.

Quinn, Naomi & Jeanette Marie Mageo (eds.). (2013), *Attachment Reconsidered: Cultural Perspectives on a Western Theory*, New York: Palgrave Macmillan.

Reis, Ricardo (2018), Is something really wrong with macroeconomics? *Oxford Review of Economic Policy* 31(1–2): 132–55.

Richard, Analiese & Daromir Rudnyckj (2009), Economies of affect, *Journal of the Royal Anthropological Institute* 15(1): 57–77.

Romer, Paul (2016), 'The trouble with macroeconomics', delivered 5 January 2016 at the Commons Memorial Lecture of the Omicron Delta Epsilon Society.

Rosenberg, Alex & Tyer Curtain (2013), What is economics good for? *New York Times*, 26 August 2013, page SR9.

Ross, Norbert (2004), *Culture and Cognition: Implications for Theory and Method*, Thousand Oaks, CA: Sage.

Rutherford, Malcolm (2001), Institutional economics: Then and now, *Journal of Economic Perspectives* 15(3): 173–94.

Sahlins, Marshall (1976), *Culture and Practical Reason*, Chicago: University of Chicago Press.

Sanfrey, Alan G. et al. (2006), Neuroeconomics: Cross-currents in research on decision-making, *Trends in Cognitive Science*, 10(3): 108–16.

Savvides, Andreas & Thanasis Stengos (2009), *Human Capital and Economic Growth*, Stanford: Stanford University Press.

Schelling, Thomas C. (1978/2006), *Micromotives and Macrobehaviour*, New York and London: W.W. Norton.

Schlefer, Jonathan (2012), *The Assumptions Economists Make*, Cambridge, MA: Harvard University Press.

Schultz, Bart (2017), *The Happiness Philosophers: The Lives and Works of the Great Utilitarians*, Princeton: Princeton University Press.

Shafir, Eldar, Itamar Simonson & Amos Tversky (1993), Reason-based choice, *Cognition* 49: 11–36.

Shih, Yi-Che, Chiu L. Chou & Wen-Yan Chiau (2010), Maritime safety for fishing boat operations and avoidable hijacking in Taiwan, *Marine Policy* 34: 349–51.

Skidelsky, Robert (2003), The mystery of growth, New York Review of Books, 13 March 2003.

Slovic, Paul, Melissa L. Finucane, Ellen Peters & Donald G. MacGregor (2004), Risk as analysis and risk as feelings: Some thoughts about affect, reason, risk, and rationality, *Risk Analysis* 24(2): 311–22.

Solow, Robert (1997), *Learning from 'Learning by Doing': Lessons for Economic Growth*, Stanford: Stanford University Press.

Sperber, Dan (1985), Apparently irrational beliefs, in *On Anthropological Knowledge*. Cambridge: Cambridge University Press, pp. 35–63.

(1997), Intuitive and reflective beliefs, *Mind and Language* 12(1): 67–83.

(2009), Culturally transmitted misbeliefs, *Behavioral and Brain Sciences* 32: 534–5.

Sperber, Dan, Fabrice Clement, Christophe Heintz, Olivier Mascaro, Hugo Mercier, Gloria Origgi & Deirdre Wilson (2010), Epistemic vigilance, *Mind and Language* 25(4): 359–93.

Stafford, Charles (1995), *The Roads of Chinese Childhood: Learning and Identification in Angang*, Cambridge: Cambridge University Press.

(2000a), *Separation and Reunion in Modern China*, Cambridge: Cambridge University Press.

(2000b), Chinese patriliny and the cycles of yang and laiwang, in Janet Carsten (ed.), *Cultures of Relatedness*, Cambridge: Cambridge University Press.

(2003), Langage et apprentissage des nombres in Chine et a Taiwan [Language and numerical learning in rural China and Taiwan], *Terrain* 40: 65–80.

(2004), Two stories of learning and economic agency in Yunnan, *Taiwan Journal of Anthropology* 2(1): 171–94.

(2006), Deception, corruption and the Chinese ritual economy, in Kevin Latham, Stuart Thompson & Jacob Klein (eds.), *Consuming China: Approaches to Cultural Change in Contemporary China*, London: Routledge.

(2007), What is going to happen next? in R. Astuti, J. Parry & C. Stafford (eds.), *Questions of Anthropology*, Oxford: Berg, pp. 55–76.

(2008a), Actually existing Chinese matriarchy, in S. Brandstadter & G. Santos (eds.), *Chinese Kinship: Contemporary Anthropological Perspectives*, Abingdon: Routledge, pp. 137–53.

(2008b), Linguistic and cultural variables in the psychology of numeracy, in M. Engelke (ed.), *The Objects of Evidence: Anthropological Approaches to the Production of Knowledge*, London: Royal Anthropological Institute, pp. S128–41.

References

(2009), Numbers and the natural history of imagining the self in Taiwan and China, *Ethnos* 74(1): 110–26.

(2010a), Some qualitative mathematics in China, *Anthropology Theory* 10(1–2): 81–6.

(2010b), The punishment of ethical behavior, in M. Lambek (ed.), *Ordinary Ethics: Anthropology, Language, and Action*, New York: Fordham University Press, pp. 187–206.

(2011a), Living with the economists, *Anthropology of This Century* 1. http://aotcpress.com/articles/living-with-economists/.

(2011b), What Confucius would make of it, *Anthropology of This Century*, Issue 2, October. http://aotcpress.com/articles/confucius-2/.

(2012), Misfortune and what can be done about it: A Taiwanese case study, *Social Analysis* 56(2): 90–102.

(2015), Being careful what you wish for: The case of happiness in China, *Hau* 5(3): 25–43.

(ed.) (2003), *Living with Separation in China*, London: Routledge/Curzon.

Swedberg, Richard (1999), Max Weber as an economist and as a sociologist: Towards a fuller understanding of Weber's view of economics, *The American Journal of Economics and Sociology* 58(4): 561–82.

Ting, Kuo-Huan, Ching-Hsiewn Ou & Wen-Hong Liu (2012), The management of the distant water tuna fishery in Taiwan, *Marine Policy* 36: 1234–41.

Tomasello, Michael (2009), *Why We Cooperate*, Cambridge, MA: MIT Press.

Toren, Christina (1990), *Making Sense of Hierarchy: Cognition as Social Process in Fiji*, London: Athlone.

(1999), *Mind, Materiality and History: Explorations in Fijian Ethnography*, London: Routledge.

van Staveren, Irene (2007), Beyond Utilitarianism and deontology: Ethics in economics, *Review of Political Economy* 19(1): 21–35.

Wade, Robert (2014), The Piketty phenomenon: Why has capital become a publishing sensation? *International Affairs* 90(5): 1069–83.

Walker, Harry & Iza Kavedzya (2015), Values of happiness, *Hau* 5(3): 1–23.

Watson, James L. (1975), Agnates and outsiders: Adoption in a Chinese lineage, *Man* (n.s.) 10(2): 293–306.

Weber, Max (1975a), Marginal utility theory and the fundamental law of psychophysics, *Social Science Quarterly* 56(1): 21–36.

(1975b), *Roscher and Knies: The Logical Problems of Historical Economics*, New York: The Free Press.

(1981), Some categories of interpretive sociology, *The Sociological Quarterly* 22(2): 151–80.

West, S. A., A. S. Griffin & A. Gardner (2007), Social semantics: Altruism, cooperation, mutualism, strong reciprocity and group selection, *Journal of Evolutionary Biology* 20(2): 415–32.

Weszkalnys, Gisa (2011), Cursed resources, or articulations of economic theory in the Gulf of Guinea, *Economy and Society* 40(3): 345–72.

Wilk, Richard (2013), Review of anthropology, economics, and choice, *Anthropology of Work Review*, 34(1): 52–3.

Wolf, Arthur (1995), *Sexual Attraction and Childhood Association*, Stanford: Stanford University Press.

(2014), *Incest Avoidance and the Incest Taboos: Two Aspects of Human Nature*, Stanford: Stanford University Press.

Wolf, Margery (1972), *Women and the Family in Rural Taiwan*, Stanford: Stanford University Press.

(1990), The woman who didn't become a shaman, *American Ethnologist* 17(3): 419–30.

Wood, Allen W. (1998), Hegel on education, in Amelie O. Rorty (ed.), *Philosophers on Education*, London: Routledge, pp. 300–17.

(2004 [1981]), *Karl Marx*, Second edition, New York & London: Routledge.

(2014), *The Free Development of Each: Studies on Freedom, Right, and Ethics in Classical German Philosophy*, Oxford: Oxford University Press.

Wren-Lewis, Simon (2015), The austerity con, *London Review of Books* 37(4): 9–11.

(2016), 'What Brexit and austerity tell us about economics, policy and the media', Sheffield Political Economy Research Institute, Paper No. 36, University of Sheffield.

Xiaotong, Fei (1992), *From the Soil: The Foundations of Chinese Society*, Berkeley: University of California Press.

Xu, Dianqing (1997), The KMT party's enterprises in Taiwan, *Modern Asian Studies* 31(2): 399–413.

Yan, Yunxiang (1993), *The Flow of Gifts: Reciprocity and Social Networks in a Chinese Village*, Stanford: Stanford University Press.

(1996), *The Flow of Gifts: Reciprocity and Social Networks in a Chinese Village*, Stanford: Stanford University Press.

(2003), *Private Life under Socialism*, Stanford: Stanford University Press.

(2013), The drive for success and the ethics of the striving individual, in Charles Stafford (ed.), *Ordinary Ethics in China*, London: Bloomsbury, pp. 263–91.

(2016), Old and new moralities in changing china, Anthropology of This Century, Issue 15, http://aotcpress.com.

Zafirovski, Milan (2001), Max Weber's analysis of marginal utility theory and psychology revisited: Latent propositions in economic sociology and the sociology of economics, *History of Political Economy* 33(3): 437–58.

Index

Index

Index

Printed in Great Britain
by Amazon